# CONNECTING WITH
# GOD

## A SPIRITUAL FORMATION GUIDE

A RENOVARÉ RESOURCE

FOR INDIVIDUALS AND GROUPS

*Introduction by Richard J. Foster*

*Lynda L. Graybeal and Julia L. Roller*

HarperOne
*A Division of HarperCollinsPublishers*

HarperOne

*Designed by Sharon VanLoozenoord*

Library of Congress Cataloging-in-Publication Data is available.

ISBN: 978–0–06–084123–2

07 08 09 10 11 RRD(H) 10 9 8 7 6 5

# CONTENTS

# INTRODUCTION

For five years I engaged in what is bound to be my life's richest adventure of biblical work. Five of us (in time to be called general editors) were wrestling with the whole of Scripture through the lens of spiritual formation, seeing what we could learn and how we could be formed and conformed and transformed ever more deeply in the subterranean chambers of the soul. That project eventually came into published form as *The Renovaré Spiritual Formation Bible*.

How do I describe to you the excitement of those early days? To be sure, it was genuine work, for the intensity of labor was exhausting, but it was so much more than "work." It was the thrill of creative ideas flying fast and furious, of dynamic insights crammed one upon another. In those chaotic sessions I often felt like I was astride a wild stallion at full gallop, gripping the mane for dear life.

But it wasn't just the excitement of new concepts emerging out of the wealth of pooled intellectual capital. No, it was the sense of awe before the majesty of Scripture, of being drawn in toward the Divine Center, of holy stillness, of quiet worship and whispered promptings. And prayers—morning prayers and evening prayers and days soaked in prayerful sharing over the sacred text. Oh yes, and laughter. Deep, side-splitting belly laughter. Holy hilarity I guess you could call it.

The experience was joyfully creative and soul-expanding. We knew we were onto something big—big ideas with huge consequences for the hearts and minds of precious people.

At some point in this dynamic process we began to ask if a way could be found to help those who would read this *Renovaré Bible* to experience something of the excitement and adventure we had in first hammering out the concepts of the "Immanuel Principle" and the "with-God life." Could others discover for themselves how the "with-God" framework illuminates God's purposes in history? How over many centuries and through multiple human authors, God has so superintended the development of the Bible that it speaks to us about real life (*zoë*) and teaches us how to live "with God" through the vicissitudes of human experience? How the aim of God in history is the creation of an all-inclusive community of loving persons, with God himself included in this community as its prime sustainer and most glorious inhabitant? How the unity of the Bible is discovered in the lived community reality of this *zoë* life under God and with God and through the power of God?

And so these spiritual formation guides were born. Together they will take us on a journey through the entire panorama of Scripture. Through these spiritual formation guides, we will discover how the Old Testament depicts God's pursuit of loving relationship with his chosen people, Israel, and how through Israel all the peoples of the earth are to be blessed. We see this "pursuit of loving relationship" carried on through the lives of the patriarchs, the history of the Israelites in their exodus from slavery and their entrance into the Promised Land, in the forming and then the disintegration of tribe and nation. Then, the New Testament depicts the story of God's fulfillment of "loving relationship" with a people who become God's own through their identity in Jesus Christ: "God's household, having been built upon the foundation of the apostles and prophets, Christ Jesus Himself being the corner *stone,* in whom the whole building, being fitted together, is growing into a holy temple in the Lord; in whom you also are being built together into a dwelling of God in the Spirit" (Eph 2:19–22, NASB).

As the Bible closes, it opens a window onto the fulfillment of God's purposes for humanity beyond human history: "Now the dwelling of God is with human beings, and he will live with them. They will be his people, and God himself will be with them and be their God" (Rev 21:3, NIVI).

Thus, we will discover that the Immanuel Principle is, after all, a cosmic principle that God has used all along in creation and redemption. It alone serves to guide human life aright on earth now and even illuminates the future of the universe. Of course, the few examples I have shared here hardly touch the surface of the great river of life that flows from God through Scripture and into the thirsty wastelands of the human soul. "Let anyone who is thirsty come to me [Jesus] and drink. Whoever believes in me, as the Scripture has said, will have streams of living water flowing from within" (John 7:37–38, NIVI).

This study guide, therefore, has been created to help each of us enter into the story of the Bible so as to see our own story, our own journey in the great cosmic drama of divine-human relationship. May you, may I, choose to surrender freely to this river of life, receiving and helping others to receive this Life, this *Zoë,* as our own.

*Richard J. Foster*

# HOW TO USE THIS GUIDE

This book is dedicated to nurturing spiritual formation through the study of Scripture. Devotional excerpts from the writings of ancient and contemporary Christians; questions for reflection; and exercises centered around Spiritual Disciplines, such as study, prayer, solitude, meditation, and silence; supplement and illumine the biblical text. This book is not intended to be read passively; it requires the interactive participation of you the reader. To engage with the texts we have chosen and to do the exercises we have set out here will require time and dedication beyond mere reading of the guide. We hope you will accept this challenge!

Whether you are using the guide as an individual or as a group, we recommend that you begin by reading "The With-God Life" and becoming familiar with the accompanying chart, which will give you some insight into the role of Scripture in the process of spiritual formation. Then you should read the Overview, which will give you a sense of the main themes we discuss. The material in the chapters of this guide is intended to help you take the next step—to engage in activities that will help you grow closer to God.

## INSTRUCTIONS FOR INDIVIDUALS

Because this book is an interactive guide for spiritual formation, we recommend that you read it more slowly than you would another kind of book. Read the Devotional and Scripture Readings and the My Life with God Exercise at the beginning of each chapter, then try to give yourself at least a week to do the exercise before reading the rest of the chapter. You may want to use a journal or notebook to record your responses to the questions in the chapter. Move on to a new chapter when you feel ready.

## INSTRUCTIONS FOR GROUPS

If this is your first time participating in a spiritual formation group, your first question is likely: What is a spiritual formation group, anyway? Simply put, a spiritual formation group consists of two to seven people who meet together on a regular basis, bringing challenge and focus to their spiritual lives. Through mutual encouragement and accountability, spiritual formation groups enable their members to assist one another on the road of discipleship to Jesus Christ. We need encouragement during the times when we succeed and the times when we fail in our life of discipleship. We need others to keep us accountable, to remind us to continually pursue our lives with God and our discipleship to Jesus. Each is a natural by-product of the spiritual formation group experience.

If you are just starting a group, try recruiting one or two friends and asking each to recruit one other person. You could also place an ad in your church bulletin or make an announcement at your weekly service. Try to limit your group to seven people or fewer. With a larger group, meetings tend to run too long and not all members participate equally. Four or five people is optimal.

Plan for at least twelve group meetings, each dedicated to a chapter. (You might choose to have an additional introductory meeting or an extra final meeting for evaluation and making future plans.) Meet as often as once a week or as infrequently as once a month, whatever is best for your group. Each meeting should last sixty to ninety minutes. Although you may want to designate someone to be in charge of initial logistics and communication about meeting times and places, we have designed these guides to work in a leaderless format. Each week a different person serves as a facilitator to keep the discussion moving along. No extra study or preparation is required for that person; he or she simply follows the group directions in the margin of each chapter.

**Before the first meeting,** each member should read the Devotional and Scripture Readings and do the My Life with God Exercise in the first chapter. Because of these requirements and to make group meetings easier, it is helpful for each member of the group to have their own copy of this book. Members read ahead in this way before every meeting. The exercises are quite involved and require a time commitment of at least a few minutes each day over several days. Allow at least a week for members to do the exercise before holding the first meeting. Some may wish to read through the entire chapter beforehand, but it is not necessary to do so.

At the end of each chapter are additional exercises, resources, and reflection questions. These optional sections are primarily intended for individual use after the group meeting. Some may enjoy writing out answers to reflection questions in the extra space provided or in their journals or notebooks. But if your group is quite interested in a particular chapter, you might consider incorporating the Additional Reflection Questions into your group meeting.

Now you are ready to form your group and plan your first meeting! May God bless you richly in this endeavor.

*Lynda L. Graybeal and Julia L. Roller*

# THE WITH-GOD LIFE

*Adapted from an essay in* The Renovaré Spiritual Formation Bible *by Gayle Beebe, Richard J. Foster, Lynda L. Graybeal, Thomas C. Oden, and Dallas Willard*

## CATCHING THE VISION: THE LIFE

The Bible is all about human life "with God." It is about how God has made this "with-God" life possible and will bring it to pass. In fact, the name Immanuel, meaning in Hebrew "God is with us," is the title given to the one and only Redeemer because it refers to God's everlasting intent for human life—namely, that we should be in every aspect a dwelling place of God. *Indeed, the unity of the Bible is discovered in the development of life with God as a reality on earth, centered in the person of Jesus.* We might call this the *Immanuel Principle* of life.

This dynamic, pulsating, with-God life is on nearly every page of the Bible. To the point of redundancy, we hear that *God is with* his people: with Abraham and Moses, with Esther and David, with Isaiah, Jeremiah, Amos, Micah, Haggai, and Malachi, with Mary, Peter, James, and John, with Paul and Barnabas, with Priscilla and Aquila, with Lydia, Timothy, Epaphroditus, Phoebe, and with a host of others too numerous to name.

Accordingly, the primary purpose of the Renovaré guides is to enable us to see and understand the reality of the "with-God" life, to enter the process of the transformation of our whole person and of our whole life into *Christlikeness.*

### Opening Ourselves to the Life

If we want to receive from the Bible the life "with God" that is portrayed *in* the Bible, we must be prepared to have our dearest and most fundamental assumptions about ourselves and our associations called into question. We must read humbly and in a constant attitude of repentance. Only in this way can we gain a thorough and practical grasp of the spiritual riches that God has made available to all humanity in his written Word.

When we turn to Scripture in this way, our reason for "knowing" the Bible and everything it teaches is that we might love more and know more of love.

or float upon it
going where it
takes you

We experience this love not as an abstraction but as a practical reality that possesses us. And because all those who love thoroughly obey the law, we would become ever more obedient to Jesus Christ and his Father.

Our goal is not to control the Bible—that is, to try to make it "come out right"—but simply to release its life into our lives and into our world. We seek to trust the living water that flows from Christ through the Bible, to open ourselves to this living water and to release it into the world as best we can, and then get out of its way.

## NURTURING THE INTENTION: THE BIBLE

God remains with the Bible always. It is God's book. No one owns it but God himself. It is the loving heart of God made visible and plain. And receiving this message of exquisite love is the great privilege of all who long for life with God. *Reading, studying, memorizing, and meditating upon Scripture has always been the foundation of the Christian disciplines.* All of the disciplines are built upon Scripture. Our practice of the Spiritual Disciplines is kept on course by our immersion in Scripture. And so it is, we come to see, that this reading, studying, memorizing, and meditating is totally in the service of "the life which is life indeed" (1 Tim 6:19, RSV). We long with all our heart to know *for ourselves* this with-God kind of life that Jesus brings in all its fullness.

And the Bible has been given to help us. God has so superintended the writing of Scripture that it serves as a most reliable guide for our spiritual formation. But God uses human action in its presentation to the world, just as it is authored by humans. Thus we must consider how we ourselves can come to the Bible and also how we can present it to all peoples in a way that inducts the soul into the eternal kind of life.

We begin by finding experientially, day by day, how to let Jesus Christ live in every dimension of our being. In Christian community, we can open our lives to God's life by gathering regularly in little groups of two or more to encourage one another to discover the footprints of God in our daily existence and to venture out *with God* into areas where we have previously walked alone or not at all.

But the aim is not external conformity, whether to doctrine or deed, but the re-formation of the inner self—of the spiritual core, the place of thought and feeling, of will and character. The psalmist cries, "You desire truth in the inward being; therefore teach me wisdom in my secret heart. . . . Create in me a clean heart, O God, and put a new and right spirit within me" (Ps 51:6, 10). It is the "inner person" that is being "*renewed [renovaré] day by day"* (2 Cor 4:16, emphasis added).

While the many Christian traditions differ over the details of spiritual formation, they all come out at the same place: the transformation of the person into Christlikeness. "Spiritual formation" is the process of transforming the inner reality of the self (the *inward being* of the psalmist) in such a way that the overall life with God seen in the Bible naturally and freely comes to pass in us. Our inner world (the *secret heart*) becomes the home of Jesus, by his initiative and our response. As a result, our interior world becomes increasingly like the inner self of Jesus and, therefore, the natural source of words and deeds that are characteristic of him. By his enabling presence, we come to "let the same mind be in you that was in Christ Jesus" (Phil 2:5).

## UNDERSTANDING THE MEANS: THE SPIRITUAL DISCIPLINES

This "with-God" life we find in the Bible is the very life to which we are called. In fact, it is exactly the life Jesus is referring to when he declares, "I am come that they might have life, and that they might have *it* more abundantly" (John 10:10, KJV). It is a life of unhurried peace and power. It is solid. It is serene. It is simple. It is radiant. It takes no time, though it permeates all of our time.

But such a life does not simply fall into our hands. Frankly, it is no more automatic for us than it was for those luminaries who walk across the pages of the Bible. There is a God-ordained way to become the kind of people and communities that can fully and joyfully enter into such abundant living. And this involves intentionally "train[ing] ... in godliness" (1 Tim 4:7). This is the purpose of the *disciplines* of the spiritual life. Indeed, the very reason for these spiritual formation guides is so that Scripture may be the primary means for the discovery, instruction, and practice of the Spiritual Disciplines, which bring us all the more fully into the with-God life.

The Spiritual Disciplines, then, are the God-ordained means by which each of us is enabled to bring the little, individualized power-pack we all possess—we call it the human body—and place it before God as "a living sacrifice" (Rom 12:1). It is the way we go about training in the spiritual life. By means of this process we become, through time and experience, the kind of person who naturally and freely expresses "love, joy, peace, patience, kindness, generosity, faithfulness, gentleness, and self-control" (Gal 5:22–23).

### Many and Varied

What are these Spiritual Disciplines? They include fasting and prayer, study and service, submission and solitude, confession and worship, meditation and silence, simplicity, frugality, secrecy, sacrifice, and celebration. Such Spiritual Disciplines crop up repeatedly in the Bible as the way God's people trained themselves and were trained by God to achieve godliness. And not only in the Bible: the saints down through history, and even spilling over into our own time, have all practiced these ways of "grow[ing] in grace" (2 Pet 3:18).

A Spiritual Discipline is an intentionally directed action by which we do what we *can* do in order to receive from God the ability (or power) to do what we cannot achieve by direct effort. It is not in us, for example, to love our enemies. We might try very hard to love our enemies, but we will fail miserably. Always. This strength, this power to love our enemies—that is, to genuinely and unconditionally love those who curse us and spitefully use us—is simply not within our natural abilities. We cannot do it by ourselves. Ever.

But this *fact of life* does not mean that we do nothing. Far from it! Instead, by an act of the will we choose to take up disciplines of the spiritual life that we can do. These disciplines are all actions of body, mind, and spirit that are within our power. Not always and not perfectly, to be sure. But they are things we can do. By choice. By choosing actions of *fasting, study, solitude,* and so forth.

### Their Purpose

The Spiritual Disciplines in and of themselves have no merit whatsoever. They possess no righteousness, contain no rectitude. Their purpose—their only purpose—is to place us before God. After that they have come to the end of their usefulness. But it is enough. Then the grace of God steps in and takes this simple offering of ourselves and creates out of it a person who embodies the goodness of God—indeed, a person who can come to the place of truly loving even enemies.

Again, Spiritual Disciplines involve doing what we *can* do to receive from God the power to do what we cannot do. And God graciously uses this process to produce in us the kind of person who automatically will do what needs to be done when it needs to be done.

Now, this ability to do what needs to be done when it needs to be done is the true freedom in life. Freedom comes not from the absence of restraint but from the presence of discipline. When we are on the spot, when we find ourselves in the midst of a crisis, it is too late. Training in the Spiritual Disciplines is the God-ordained means for forming and transforming the human personality so that when we are in a crisis we can be "response-able"—able to respond appropriately.

## EXPERIENCING THE GRACE OF GOD:
## THE EFFORT

It is vitally important for us to see all this spiritual training in the context of the work and action of God's grace. As the great apostle Paul reminds us, "It is God who is at work in you, enabling you both to will and to work for his good pleasure" (Phil 2:13). This, you see, is no "works righteousness," as it is sometimes called. Even our desire for this "with-God" kind of life is an action of grace; it is "prevenient grace," as the theologians say. You see, we are not just saved by grace, we live by grace. We pray by grace and fast by grace and study by grace and serve by grace and worship by grace. *All the disciplines are permeated by the enabling grace of God.*

But do not misunderstand—there *are* things for us to do. Daily. Grace never means inaction or total passivity. In ordinary life we will encounter many moments of decision when we must engage the will, saying "Yes!" to God's will and to God's way, as the People of God have done throughout history.

The opposite of grace is works, not effort. "Works" have to do with earning, and there simply is nothing any of us can do to earn God's love or acceptance. And, of course, we don't have to. God already loves us utterly and perfectly, and our complete acceptance is the free gift of God through Jesus Christ our Lord. In God's amazing grace, we live and move and have our being. But if we ever hope to "grow in grace," we will find ourselves engaging in effort of the most strenuous kind. As Jesus says, we are to "*strive* to enter through the narrow door" (Luke 13:24, emphasis added). And Peter urges us to "make every *effort* to support your faith with goodness, and goodness with knowledge, and knowledge with self-control, and self-control with endurance, and endurance with godliness, and godliness with mutual affection, and mutual affection with love" (2 Pet 1:5–7, emphasis added). It is this formation—indeed transformation—that we all desire.

## TRAVELING WITH THE PEOPLE OF GOD: THE JOURNEY

The luminaries who walk across the pages of our Bible not only practiced the various and sundry Spiritual Disciplines that formed—indeed transformed—them into Christlikeness, but did so while on a journey. The Bible records their lives as they traveled from the Garden of Eden to Canaan to Egypt to the Promised Land to Babylon and back. Then Jesus instructed the People of God to be his witnesses "to the ends of the earth" (Acts 1:8c), until they arrive at their final destination, "a new heaven and new earth" (Rev 21:1). During their travels God made himself known in various ways to the People of God wherever they were and whatever their social situation. They reacted to God's initiatives in many ways, sometimes rejoicing, at other times rebelling. This journey has been identified by the general editors of *The Renovaré Spiritual Formation Bible* as fifteen expressions of the with-God life (see the following chart). The book you hold in your hands illuminates one dimension, the People of God in Individual Communion. We hope it will help you understand how God has been with his people through the ages and continues to be with us today in our journey toward "the city that has foundations, whose architect and builder is God" (Heb 11:10).

# THE PEOPLE OF GOD AND THE WITH-GOD LIFE*

| Stage of Formation | Scriptures | God's Action | Human Reaction |
|---|---|---|---|
| I. The People of God in Individual Communion | *Genesis 1–11*** | Creates, instructs, steward of a good creation, banishes, destroys, restores | Disobey, rebel, sacrifice, murder, repent, obey |
| II. The People of God Become a Family | *Genesis 12–50* | Gives promise and establishes Abrahamic covenant, makes a great people | Faith, wrestle with God, persevere |
| III. The People of God in Exodus | *Exodus, Leviticus, Numbers, Deuteronomy* | Extends mercy, grace, and deliverance from exile; delivers the Mosaic covenant/law | Obey and disobey, develop a distinctive form of ritual |
| IV. The People of God in the Promised Land | *Joshua, Judges, Ruth, 1 Samuel 1–12* | Establishes a theocracy, bequeaths the Promised Land | Inhabit the Promised Land, accept judges as mediators |
| V. The People of God as a Nation | *1 Samuel 13–31 & 2 Samuel, 1 & 2 Kings, 1 & 2 Chronicles, 1 Esdras 1* | Permits the monarchy, exalts good kings, uses secular nations for blessing | Embrace the monarchy |
| VI. The People of God in Travail | *Job, Psalms of Lament, Ecclesiastes, Lamentations, Tobit* | Permits tribulation, allows suffering to strengthen faith | Complain yet remain faithful |
| VII. The People of God in Prayer and Worship | *Psalms, Psalm 151* | Establishes liturgical worship | Praise, prayer |
| VIII. The People of God in Daily Life | *Proverbs, Ecclesiastes, Song of Solomon, Wisdom of Solomon, The Wisdom of Jesus Son of Sirach (Ecclesiasticus)* | Gives precepts for living in community | Teachable, learning, treasure beautiful words and artistic expression |
| IX. The People of God in Rebellion | *1 Kings 12–2 Kings 25:10, 2 Chronicles 10–36:19, Isaiah, Jeremiah 1–36, Hosea, Joel, Amos, Jonah, Micah, Nahum, Habakkuk, Zephaniah, Judith, Prayer of Manasseh* | Proclaims prophetic judgment and redemption, reveals his rule over all nations, promises Immanuel, uses secular nations to bring judgment | Disbelieve and reject, believe false prophets, a faithful remnant emerges |
| X. The People of God in Exile | *2 Kings 25:11–30, 2 Chronicles 36:20–23, Jeremiah 37–52, Lamentations, Ezekiel, Daniel, Obadiah, Baruch, Letter of Jeremiah, Additions to Daniel* | Judges, yet remains faithful to covenant promises | Mourn, survive, long for Jerusalem, stand for God without institutions |
| XI. The People of God in Restoration | *Ezra, Nehemiah, Esther, Daniel, Haggai, Zechariah, Malachi, Additions to Esther, 1 Esdras 2–9, & 2 Esdras, 1, 2, 3, & 4 Maccabees, Tobit, Additions to Daniel* | Regathers and redeems, restructures social life | Return, obey, rebuild, worship, pursue Messianic figure, compile Septuagint |
| XII. The People of God with Immanuel | *Matthew, Mark, Luke, John* | Sends the Son and acts with the Son | Hear and follow, resist and reject |
| XIII. The People of God in Mission | *Acts* | Sends the Holy Spirit and creates the Church | Believe and proclaim, disbelieve and persecute |
| XIV. The People of God in Community | *Romans, 1 & 2 Corinthians, Galatians, Ephesians, Philippians, Colossians, 1 & 2 Thessalonians, 1 & 2 Timothy, Titus, Philemon, Hebrews, James, 1 & 2 Peter, 1, 2, & 3 John, Jude* | Builds, nurtures, and mobilizes the Church | Become disciples of Jesus Christ and make disciples to the ends of the earth |
| XV. The People of God into Eternity | *Revelation* | Reveals infinite progress toward infinite good | Worship and praise, creativity that magnifies God |

* Text taken from *The Renovaré Spiritual Formation Bible*.
** Books are placed into categories by content, not by date of composition or type of literature.

| Type of Mediation | Locus of Mediation | Social Context | Central Individual(s) | Key Spiritual Disciplines |
|---|---|---|---|---|
| Face-to-face | Garden, field, Noah's ark | Individuals | Adam, Eve, Enoch, Noah | Practicing the Presence, confession, sacrifice, obedience/submission |
| Through the family | Tent, desert, jail | Extended families and nomadic clans | Abraham and Sarah, Isaac, Jacob, Joseph | Pilgrimage, sacrifice, chastity |
| Through God's terrifying acts and the law | Ark of the covenant, tabernacle | Nomadic tribes | Moses | Submission, silence, simplicity, worship |
| Through the conquest and learning to act with God | Shiloh, Bethel | An ethnic people with fluid leadership | Joshua, Deborah, Ruth, Samson, Gideon, Samuel | Guidance, radical obedience/submission, secrecy |
| Through the king, prophets, priests, and sacrifices | Altars, consecrated places, first (Solomonic) Temple | Political nation on the world stage | Saul, David, Hezekiah, Elijah, Elisha | Worship, prayer |
| Through suffering and the disappointments of life | Ash heap, hard circumstances of life | Individual | Job, Israel as the suffering servant | Fasting, solitude, silence, submission, service, celebration |
| Through song, prayer, worship | Jerusalem, flowering of individual experience | Nation | David | Prayer, worship, confession, celebration, meditation |
| Through wisdom | Temple, in the gate, home | Nation triumphant | Solomon | Study, guidance, celebration, meditation |
| Through the prophets and repression by the Gentiles | High places, Temple desecrated and destroyed | Nation under siege and dispersed | Isaiah, Hosea, Amos | Fasting, repentance, obedience/submission, solitude, silence, the law internalized |
| Through punishment, being a blessing to their captors | Babylon, anyplace, anytime | Ethnics abroad without a political homeland | Ezekiel, Jeremiah | Detachment, fasting, simplicity, prayer, silence, service |
| Through repentance, service, synagogue study | Rebuilt Temple, synagogue | Remnant on the international scene, ethnics in the leadership of other nations | Ezra, Cyrus the Persian, Nehemiah, Maccabees, Essenes, John the Baptist | Pilgrimage, confession, worship, study, service |
| Through the Incarnate Word and the living presence of the kingdom | Temple and synagogue, boats and hillsides, gatherings of disciples | Small groups, disciples, apostles, hostile critics | Jesus Christ Incarnate | Celebration, study, pilgrimage, submission, prayer, sacrifice, obedience, confession |
| Through the Holy Spirit, persecution, and martyrdom | Temple, synagogue, schools, riversides, public square | Jew, Gentile, house churches, abandonment of social strata | Peter, Paul | Speaking and hearing the word, sacrifice, guidance, generosity/service, fasting, prayer |
| In one another, through Scripture, teaching, preaching, prophetic utterance, pastoral care, the Holy Spirit, the sacraments | Gathered community | Community redefined by the Body of Christ, decadent Greco-Roman culture | Peter, Paul, John | Prayer, study, accountability/submission, fellowship |
| Throughout the cosmos | Focused in the New Jerusalem and extending throughout the cosmos | The Trinity and its community | God the Father, Son, and Holy Spirit; apostles, prophets | Living beyond disciplines |

# CONNECTING WITH GOD: AN OVERVIEW

An essential part of living the with-God life is learning how we are to communicate with God. From the very outset of human history, God was present with humans as individuals. God was physically present with Adam and Eve in the garden, walking with them and carrying on two-way conversations. But as the members of the human race continued to act independently of and contrary to God's purposes, they gradually distanced themselves from God. Although God is no longer physically present with us in exactly the same way as he was in the story of Adam and Eve, his Spirit, his nonphysical presence, continues to abide with us. Today as then, God communicates directly with individuals, speaking with them through the indwelling Holy Spirit, appearing to them in angelic form, instructing them in dreams, and so forth.

God still desires and intends cooperative efforts and a direct, conversational relationship with us. Very simply, we are made to be in relationship with him. To use Augustine's famous words, "Thou has made us for thyself, and we are not at rest until we find our rest in thee." Our lives find their direction only when God is present. Intimate, individual communication with God is essential to our spiritual formation; it is something we must constantly seek out. We need the full assurance of God's greatness and goodness, which comes only from his direct presence. The eternal fact of our lives is that we are constantly supported by God's direct action. But being aware of how God is supporting us and communicating with us is not always easy. We must train ourselves to listen for God and to respond to him. This is the basis of any relationship: communication, sharing, and respect. In this guide we will explore twelve ways to experience individual communion with God: living with God, prayer, Bible study, the creation, other people, circumstances, silence, dreams and visions, sensing God's presence, encountering his messengers, wrestling with God, and finally, walking with God. It is our hope that this guide will enhance your individual communion with God in this journey of the with-God life.

# 1 LIVING WITH GOD

## DEVOTIONAL READING

FRANK LAUBACH, *Letters by a Modern Mystic*

*April 22, 1930*   This morning I started out fresh, by finding a rich experience of God in the sunrise. Then I tried to let Him control my hands while I was shaving and dressing and eating breakfast. Now I am trying to let God control my hands as I pound the typewriter keys.... There is nothing that we can do excepting to throw ourselves open to God. There is, there must be, so much more in Him than He can give us.... It ought to be tremendously helpful to be able to acquire the habit of reaching out strongly after God's thoughts, and to ask, "God, what have you to put into my mind now if only I can be large enough?" That waiting, eager attitude ought to give God the chance he needs.

*May 14, 1930*   Oh, this thing of keeping in constant touch with God, of making him the object of my thought and the companion of my conversations, is the most amazing thing I ever ran across. *It is working.* I cannot do it even half a day—not yet, but I believe I shall be doing it some day for the entire day. It is a matter of acquiring a new habit of thought. Now I *like* God's presence so much that when for a half hour or so he slips out of mind—as he does many times a day—I feel as though I had deserted him, and as though I had lost something very precious in my life.[1]

> It is helpful for everyone to read the Devotional and Scripture Readings and do the My Life with God Exercise before the meeting. Begin the meeting with silent prayer, then move directly to Reflecting on My Life with God below.

## MY LIFE WITH GOD EXERCISE

Many of us make the mistake of assuming that intimate communication with God ended with biblical times. The testimony of Frank Laubach and others throughout history, including Francis of Assisi and Julian of Norwich, shows that this is a false assumption. Dallas Willard wrote in *Hearing God,*

> Today I continue to believe that people are meant to live in an ongoing conversation with God, speaking and being spoken to. Rightly understood I believe that this can be abundantly verified in experience. God's visits to Adam and Eve in the Garden, Enoch's walks with God and the face-to-face conversations between Moses and Jehovah are all commonly regarded as highly exceptional moments in the religious history of humankind. Aside from their obviously unique historical role, however, they are not meant to be exceptional at all. Rather they are examples of the normal human life God intended for us: God's indwelling his people through personal presence and fellowship. Given who we are by basic nature, we live—really live—only through God's regular speaking in our souls and thus "by every word that comes from the mouth of God."[2]

We may no longer be able to literally live with God in the garden, but we have available to us many other methods of conversing with him. Make a list of the ways you communicate with God—for example, worship, Bible study, receiving communion, prayer. This week try to be aware of all the times you communicate with the Creator, adding to your list as you think of new ideas. Some may surprise you. You might find that you are connecting with God when you have a conversation with good friends, when you admire a sunset, or even when you complain about a task you don't like doing. Think about your patterns of communication. Are you often alone when you find yourself talking with God or do you find yourself connecting with God most easily when you are around others? Does quiet help? Does being outdoors make a difference? QT on my walk.

As the week progresses, consider what, if anything, may be hindering your communication with God. For example, our motives for seeking to hear from God may not be the right ones. We should not seek God as we would a fortune-teller, to be assured of our future or our own comfort. Nor should we seek to hear God so we can brag about it to others. Moreover, our communication with God can be impaired if we misunderstand God's nature and his intent for us. God desires relationship with us, not to be our puppet master. He wishes to guide us, not to make all our decisions for us. Think about each of these. Are any of these attitudes, or another obstacle, hindering your fellowship with God?

God putting thoughts of people in my mind. I pray immediately.

But I am alone a lot

*Verbal, a hand upon my heart, a giving over*

*What were some of the ways you found yourself communicating with God? What obstacles to that conversation did you identify?* Straying thoughts, believing lies & whispers

**REFLECTING ON MY LIFE WITH GOD**
Allow each member a few moments to answer this question.

## ▶ SCRIPTURE READING: GENESIS 3:1–13

Now the serpent was more crafty than any other wild animal that the LORD God had made. He said to the woman, "Did God say, 'You shall not eat from any tree in the garden'?" The woman said to the serpent, "We may eat of the fruit of the trees in the garden; but God said, 'You shall not eat of the fruit of the tree that is in the middle of the garden, nor shall you touch it, or you shall die.'" But the serpent said to the woman, "You will not die; for God knows that when you eat of it your eyes will be opened, and you will be like God, knowing good and evil." So when the woman saw that the tree was good for food, and that it was a delight to the eyes, and that the tree was to be desired to make one wise, she took of its fruit and ate; and she also gave some to her husband, who was with her, and he ate. Then the eyes of both were opened, and they knew that they were naked; and they sewed fig leaves together and made loincloths for themselves.

They heard the sound of the LORD God walking in the garden at the time of the evening breeze, and the man and his wife hid themselves from the presence of the LORD God among the trees of the garden. But the LORD God called to the man, and said to him, "Where are you?" He said, "I heard the sound of you in the garden, and I was afraid, because I was naked; and I hid myself." He said, "Who told you that you were naked? Have you eaten from the tree of which I commanded you not to eat?" The man said, "The woman whom you gave to be with me, she gave me fruit from the tree, and I ate." Then the LORD God said to the woman, "What is this that you have done?" The woman said, "The serpent tricked me, and I ate."

After everyone has had a chance to respond to the question, ask a member to read this passage from Scripture.

*What stands out to you upon hearing this familiar passage?*

**REFLECTION QUESTION**
Allow each person a few moments to respond to this question.

## ▶▶ GETTING THE PICTURE

The story of Adam and Eve begins with an idyllic life in the garden. When it becomes apparent that Adam is going to be lonely, God makes a companion for him, one who shares his privileges and duties. Together

After a brief discussion, choose one person to read this section.

they have dominion over the whole of the plant and animal kingdom. Adam and Eve's only work is to take care of the garden, which provides all the food they need.

Not only does the LORD God provide for Adam and Eve's physical needs, but he also becomes their companion. He speaks to them on a variety of topics, from pronouncing a blessing upon them to giving them instructions about what they can and cannot eat in the garden (1:28ff and 2:16–17). The only biblical record of any response, before the account we just read, from either Adam or Eve is Adam's exclamation when God brings Eve to him:

> This at last is bone of my bones
>     and flesh of my flesh;
> this one shall be called Woman,
>     for out of Man this one was taken. (2:23)

We can surmise that God gave Adam and Eve instruction on a variety of subjects, and in the Scripture Reading, we have more than instruction or guidance. This passage describes a two-way conversation, through which we can glimpse the intimate conversations that took place. The story suggests that God is physically present with Adam and Eve, perhaps even face-to-face. Adam and Eve actually hear the sound of God walking in the garden and then physically hide themselves from him, ashamed of their newly discovered nakedness and embarrassed by their disobedience. He still calls to them, however, and draws out of them the story of their disobedience.

## ▶▶▶ GOING DEEPER

✍ Have another member read this section.

The conversation God had with Adam and Eve hardly represents humankind's proudest moment. Adam and Eve had just deliberately disobeyed the only rule they were given, and they promptly blamed everyone else for their disobedience, including God (although indirectly—"The woman whom *you* gave" [Gen 3:12, emphasis added]). How many of us have imagined what we would have done if we had been there? It is easy to think from a distance that we would have rejected that proffered fruit. That Adam and Eve blew it big-time. They had everything, didn't they? Companionship, food, meaningful work, face-to-face conversation with God. But before we get too critical of Adam and Eve, as they hide among the trees after their one terrible mistake, picture God looking for *us* in the garden, fully cognizant of all of our flaws and failures. How far would we run?

Like us, Adam and Eve were given the gift of freedom—the freedom to make their own choices, even the freedom to throw away all of God's other good gifts. What they did not have, however, was an understanding of the power of freedom. They did not know the consequences of actions that conflicted with God's plan for their lives. They did not yet have the character to handle the knowledge of good and evil provided by eating fruit from the forbidden tree. God's relationship with them was one of guidance and apprenticeship. The purpose of his conversations with Adam and Eve was to form their characters, to teach them how to handle the responsibility of their freedom to make choices, so that they could work in companionship with him. Having been created as fully formed adults, Adam and Eve had bypassed the process of having their characters and spirits formed in the context of a family or religious community. So God gave them instructions about how to live. Subdue the earth but take care of it. Have dominion over the animals but be friends with them. Fill the earth with your progeny. Eat from the plants and trees. Till the garden so you will have plenty to eat. In your freedom, cooperate with me to make this a successful enterprise. Then and now, God has no interest in robots. He gave instructions but did not force Adam and Eve to obey them.

Their characters, like ours, could be formed only by God allowing them to make choices in response to what he put before them. And this left the possibility of disastrous results. When they made the wrong choice, they had to face the consequences, and so do we. Yet the very fact of their disobedience makes the subsequent conversation all the more remarkable. God still sought them out. God knew of their disobedience; he also knew they were hiding. Yet God called out to them, gave them both a chance to confess to him. Their defiant act did not end the learning; the conversations continue, even into future generations, although at a greater distance.

*What does Adam and Eve's interaction with God teach us about our own communication with God?*

**REFLECTION QUESTION**
Allow each person a few moments to respond.

## ▶▶▶ POINTING TO GOD

Adam and Eve's expulsion from the garden in no way marked the end of intimate, one-to-one conversation with God. The Bible contains numerous stories of such conversations, but there are also many modern

✍ Choose one member to read this section.

examples. Before he wrote the journal entries in this chapter's Devotional Reading, Frank Laubach had an experience in which he believed God spoke to him through Laubach's own mouth. Laubach was working as a missionary in Mindanao, a remote island in the Philippines. This area was considered so isolated and dangerous that Laubach's family stayed behind in a larger city. Alone, Laubach became discouraged with his initial lack of progress. The people he was working with were Muslim and deeply skeptical of Christianity. One night Laubach climbed a hill behind his cottage and sat, brooding over his lack of success. There he had a life-changing experience of communication with God:

> My lips began to move and it seemed to me that God was speaking.
> "My Child," my lips said, "you have failed because you do not really love these Moros. You feel superior to them because you are white. If you can forget you are an American and think only how I love them, they will respond."
> I answered back to the sunset, "God, I don't know whether you spoke to me through my lips, but if you did, it was the truth."[3]

Laubach described the experience as erasing his prejudice and making him color-blind. Not only did it rejuvenate his ministry, it marked the beginning of Laubach's journey toward the goal of staying constantly in touch with God.

## ▶▶▶▶▶ GOING FORWARD

*Have another person read this section.*

The individual with-God life is all about pursuing a close relationship with God like the one he had with Adam and Eve in the garden. Just like Adam and Eve, we live in a world where we are tempted to do many things that aren't good for us or for those we love. Often, we make the wrong choice. Yet the guidance and instruction we receive from God through reading and studying Scripture, talking with him, listening to him, and walking with him helps form our spirits so that we will be able to respond like we should when confronted with challenges and problems. But communicating with God is much more than just knowing what to do in difficult situations. The better our communication becomes, the closer we approach Frank Laubach's goal of staying constantly in touch with him, of *living* with God. Then we can better ask Laubach's question: "God, what have you to put into my mind now if only I can be large enough?"

*What does living with God mean to you?*

**REFLECTION QUESTION**
Again, allow each member a few moments to answer this question.

This concludes our look at living with God. In the next chapter we will turn our attention to another avenue of connecting with God—prayer.

⚐ After everyone has had a chance to respond, the leader reads this paragraph.

## CLOSING PRAYER

To you, O LORD, I lift up my soul.
Make me to know your ways, O LORD;
    teach me your paths.
Lead me in your truth, and teach me,
    for you are the God of my salvation,
    for you I wait all day long.
"Come," my heart says, "seek his face!"
    Your face, LORD, do I seek.
Give ear to my words, O LORD;
    give heed to my sighing.
Listen to the sound of my cry,
    my King and my God,
    for to you I pray. Amen. (PSS 25:1, 4–5; 27:8; 5:1–2)

⚐ Allow some time for members to encourage one another to read the Devotional and Scripture Readings and do the exercise in the following chapter before the next meeting. Then invite the members to be silent for a few moments before leading them in reading the Closing Prayer aloud together.

⚐ At the end of the Closing Prayer, the leader asks for a volunteer to lead the next meeting.

## TAKING IT FURTHER

**ADDITIONAL EXERCISE**

Like Adam and Eve, Christians today are still meant to live in conversational relationship with God. Yet many of us spend much or even all of our prayer time talking to God, rather than listening for him. Think about your own prayer life. Are you listening for the voice of God or do you find that your conversations are mostly one-way? This week make a special effort to balance your words to God with periods of listening for his responses, his guidance.

**ADDITIONAL RESOURCES**

Brother Lawrence. *The Practice of the Presence of God.* New Kensington, PA: Whitaker House, 1982.
Brother Lawrence and Frank Laubach. *Practicing His Presence.* Goleta, CA: Christian Books, 1963.

Laubach, Frank C. *Letters by a Modern Mystic.* Syracuse, NY: New
Readers Press, 1979.
Willard, Dallas. *Hearing God.* 3d ed. Downers Grove, IL: InterVarsity,
1999.

ADDITIONAL REFLECTION
QUESTIONS

*We read that Adam and Eve could hear God approaching. Their hiding
implies that they could see God, or at least that he could see them. What
senses do you use to intuit God's presence? Can you sometimes feel or hear
him? If so, in what ways?*

*This privilege of face-to-face communication with God, which Adam and
Eve had and lost, is our natural state of being. Imagine for a moment a life
of constant fellowship with God. Is the idea blissful? Is it a little intimidat-
ing? What might that type of fellowship change about your life?*

*After Adam and Eve committed the first sin by disobeying God, they hid from him. Sin obscures God from our view. Think of a time when you made a wrong choice that changed the course of your life. What could you have done to avoid it? What did you have to do to correct it? Did you talk with God about it? Take a few minutes to reflect. Are any ongoing sins, or sins from your past, affecting your fellowship with God?*

# TALKING WITH GOD

## 2

## DEVOTIONAL READING

JEAN-NICHOLAS GROU, *How to Pray*

Be *simple* in your piety. Do not rely upon your intellect or upon the subtlety and depth of your reasonings. Real piety is not concerned with thoughts but with the affections. Do not use so many books and exercises and methods. Let your heart tell you what you wish to say to God and say it simply without bothering too much about the words; it is ridiculous to be eloquent in his presence and take a pride in prayers that are well composed, instead of using those that are more natural to you.

Simplicity is the characteristic of all real prayer and nothing pleases God better. He does not want so much formality in his service; great harm has been done by the reduction of devotion to a fine art dependent on so many rules. After all, everything depends on the Holy Spirit; it is he alone who teaches the true way of conversing with God and we see how, when he lays hold of a soul, the first thing he does is to withdraw it from all the rules made by men.

Lastly, be docile to the promptings of the Holy Spirit. To this end study carefully, but without too much curiosity, what happens in your heart and when you feel grace moving you, respond to it. The wind bloweth where it listeth; but when it blows the soul must not set up the least resistance; its duty is to let itself be carried where it is taken.[1]

> It is helpful for everyone to read the Devotional and Scripture Readings and do the My Life with God Exercise before the meeting. Begin the meeting with silent prayer, then move directly to Reflecting on My Life with God below.

## MY LIFE WITH GOD EXERCISE

More has probably been written about prayer than any other topic of the spiritual life. Richard Foster writes in *Prayer: Finding the Heart's True Home* that he almost gave up writing the book because there was so much material to read, so many opinions to consider, and so many varieties of prayer to study. How many methods of prayer have you tried? What are they? Some people find it helpful to use short acronyms so that they don't forget anything, for example, PRAY—Praise God for all he has done, *Repent* of your sins, *Admit* that you need him, and *Yield* the power to him—or ACTS, *Adoration, Confession, Thanksgiving,* and *Supplication* or intercession. Or perhaps you have prayed the Jesus Prayer, "Lord Jesus Christ, Son of God, have mercy on me, a sinner." Maybe you have used the words *Kyrie Eleison* (Lord, have mercy) by themselves or set to music, as a prayer or to open your prayer time. Numerous people recommend that we exclusively pray the Lord's Prayer, use it as a model for our prayers, or pray it before personal prayers to the Lord. Others use one of the psalms, often Psalm 23, to open their time with God, or prayers from the *Book of Common Prayer* or other denominational publications.

Another method is contemplative prayer. A common way to practice contemplative prayer is to sit in silence for a predetermined amount of time, quieting our hearts and minds to allow room for God. Contemplative prayer creates the emotional and spiritual space that allows Christ to construct an inner sanctuary in our hearts. It is helpful to return to a phrase, such as "Jesus," "Lord God," or "Abba," over and over, to focus and center the mind when distractions interfere with filling our minds with God.

Before the next meeting, choose a method of prayer that you are less familiar with and experiment with it. You could also experiment with different locales (at home, in your backyard, in a park, or in a stairwell in your office building) and with different prayer postures (standing, seated, on your knees, lying prostrate). It may help to keep track of your practice in a journal, noting your results with each type of prayer. Since this is an experiment, don't feel bad if you find a particular type of prayer difficult. The whole purpose of experiments is to find what brings us closer to God and what doesn't. Each of us has different spiritual strengths and preferences.

**REFLECTING ON MY LIFE WITH GOD**
Allow each member a few moments to answer this question.

*What type of prayer did you try and how did your experience go? Did you feel that the exercise supported Grou's statement that "simplicity is the characteristic of all real prayer and nothing pleases God better"?*

After everyone has had a chance to respond to the question, ask a member to read this passage from Scripture.

► **SCRIPTURE READING:** MATTHEW 6:5–13

"And whenever you pray, do not be like the hypocrites; for they love to stand and pray in the synagogues and at the street corners, so that they may be seen by others. Truly I tell you, they have received their reward.

But whenever you pray, go into your room and shut the door and pray to your Father who is in secret; and your Father who sees in secret will reward you.

"When you are praying, do not heap up empty phrases as the Gentiles do; for they think that they will be heard because of their many words. Do not be like them, for your Father knows what you need before you ask him.

"Pray then in this way:

> Our Father in heaven,
>> hallowed be your name.
>> Your kingdom come.
>> Your will be done,
>>> on earth as it is in heaven.
>> Give us this day our daily bread.
>> And forgive us our debts,
>>> as we also have forgiven our debtors.
>> And do not bring us to the time of trial,
>> but rescue us from the evil one.

For if you forgive others their trespasses, your heavenly Father will also forgive you; but if you do not forgive others, neither will your Father forgive your trespasses."

*When have you found yourself guilty of praying to try to impress others with your piety or eloquence, or found yourself heaping up empty phrases? How can these prayer traps be avoided?* Praying a sermon

**REFLECTION QUESTION** Allow each person a few moments to respond to this question.

## ▶▶ GETTING THE PICTURE

This passage comes from what we call the Sermon on the Mount, perhaps one of the best known Scriptures for Christians. Before delivering this sermon, Jesus has been baptized and identified as the Son of God by a voice from heaven and then led by the Spirit into the wilderness for forty days and nights, after which he is tempted by the devil (Matt 3:13–4:10). Then he begins his ministry in Galilee. In accordance with the teaching tradition of the rabbis, Jesus proclaims the good news of the kingdom. In addition, he cures disease and sickness among the people, spreading his fame. Great crowds of people from Galilee in the north and the Decapolis in the

After a brief discussion, choose one person to read this section.

*Talking with God*

15

northeast to Jerusalem and Judea in the south and the other side of the Jordan River in the east come to be with him and hear him (Matt 4:12–25).

When Jesus sees the crowds, he climbs a mountain, gathers his disciples around him, and begins to teach (Matt 5:1). His first teaching, which has become known as the Beatitudes, shocks the crowd, since he blesses not those usually singled out for blessings—those who carefully keep the law, the teachers and leaders—but the least honored people in Jewish society: for example, those who are poor in spirit, meek, or persecuted (Matt 5:1–12). Jesus continues to turn things upside down, as he discusses issues like anger, adultery, divorce, oaths, retaliation, and love of one's enemies. In each case, he refers to the law—"You have heard that it was said"—but then redefines the law according to the life that he is introducing to the crowds (Matt 5:21–48). Having touched on the issues that wreak the most havoc in society and the world, Jesus turns his attention to those who perform religious actions solely to receive recognition from their peers, describing the correct motivations for contributing money, praying, and fasting. Jesus cautions people not to make prayer a theatrical event and suggests a model prayer.

## ▶▶▶ GOING DEEPER

*Have another member read this section.*

Jesus taught that the condition of the heart is the most important aspect of prayer. Jesus did not say that we shouldn't pray in public but that our intention in praying should never be the praise and adoration of others. In *The Divine Conspiracy*, Dallas Willard writes, "Desire for religious respect or reputation will *immediately* drag us into the rightness of the scribes and Pharisees because that desire always focuses entirely upon the visible action, not on the source of action in the heart."[2] The heart that seeks after God does not need to seek the approval of others, regardless of how many times the person is called on to pray in public or how often they pray in private.

Public prayer, praying as a church community, or praying in small groups is important and powerful, but for our spiritual formation we cannot do better than the kind of prayer Jesus advocated—secret, solitary prayer. Praying in private centers our mind and heart on the object of our prayers alone. It strips away all pretenses. Theatrics are futile with God; we cannot make him think we are more pious than we really are. When we go into a room and shut the door to pray, we face our own naked souls in all of their sin and beauty, and gradually our focus shifts from ourselves to God.

Jesus also advocated simplicity in prayer, just as Grou emphasized: "Simplicity is the characteristic of all real prayer." At the same time, Jesus's prayer is profound, revealing an intimate knowledge of God the Father. Whereas the prayers of the Gentiles were long and empty, the Lord's Prayer is short and pithy. In it we see Jesus speaking heart-to-heart with God about ordinary, daily things: who the Father is, the coming of God's rule on earth, food, sin, and temptation. Even within the prayer itself, we see the need for right intention. The prayer begins with praise and honor to God, followed by a wish to align our will to his own. Only then do we move on to our individual needs. The last two verses remind us of the importance of the condition of our hearts: only as we forgive others will God the Father forgive us.

Jesus's prayer is devoid of pretense or posturing: he was talking with the Father about what concerned them both. This is prayer's simplest definition: talking with God about what we're doing together. To be able to talk with God is God's gift to us, a gift that develops our character and forms our spirit so that we become more and more like him—thinking like him, seeing the world through his eyes, feeling like him, loving like him. When that happens, we can work with him to bring about the good life that he desires for all of his creation. This two-way conversation between us and our lover, God, will continue as long as we willingly initiate it.

*Since prayer has been part of the human experience from the beginning, why do you think we have made the simple act of prayer so difficult?*

**REFLECTION QUESTION**
Allow each person a few moments to respond.

Sin — we think by adding more or being more eloquent, God hears us more + will respond accordingly

## ▶▶▶▶ POINTING TO GOD

Eighteenth-century British evangelist George Müller exemplifies the practice of prayer as talking to God about their work together. Müller developed a deep love of prayer early in life. When he was in seminary, he found the prayers he said in his room each night to be a "communion with God so sweet" that he would often continue praying until the wee hours of the morning and then rise early to pray again. After he finished seminary, he and his wife founded several orphanages in Bristol, caring for up to two thousand children at a time. The orphanages were funded solely by voluntary offerings, and Müller and his wife were often desperately short of money. Yet they placed their work completely in the Lord's hands, and he provided for them every time. These brief journal entries

✒ Choose one member to read this section.

demonstrate the remarkable extent to which Müller's practice of prayer allowed him to rely on the Lord:

Nov. 21, 1838.—Never were we so reduced in funds as to-day. There was not a single half-penny in hand between the matrons of the three houses. Nevertheless there was a good dinner, and by managing so as to help one another with bread, etc., there was a prospect of getting over this day also; but for none of the houses had we the prospect of being able to take in bread. When I left the brethren and sisters at one o'clock, after prayer, I told them that we must wait for help, and see how the Lord would deliver us this time. I was sure of help, but we were indeed straitened. When I came to Kingsdown, I felt that I needed more exercise, being very old; wherefore I went on the nearest way home, but round by Clarence Place. About twenty yards from my house, I met a brother who walked back with me, and after a little conversation gave me £10 to be handed over to the brethren, the deacons, towards providing the poor saints with coals, blankets and warm clothing; also £5 for the Orphans, and £5 for the other objects of the Scriptural Knowledge Institution. The brother had called twice while I was gone to the Orphan-Houses, and had I now been *one half minute* later, I should have missed him. But the Lord knew our need, and therefore allowed me to meet him. I sent off the £5 immediately to the matrons....

July 12, 1854.—Our means were now again reduced to about £30, as only about £150 had come in since June 15. In addition to this, we had very heavy expenses before us. This morning, in reading through the book of Proverbs, when I came to chapter xxii.19—'That thy trust may be in the Lord, &c.,' I said in prayer to Him: 'Lord, I do trust in Thee; but wilt Thou now be pleased to help me; for I am in need of means for the current expenses of all the various objects of the Institution.' By the first delivery of letters I received an order on a London bank for £100, to be used for all the various objects 'as the present need might require.'[3]

## ▶▶▶▶ GOING FORWARD

🖎 Have another person read this section.

George Müller's journal entries summarize beautifully the fruit of a committed prayer relationship with God. We know that he spent a great deal of time talking with God about what they were doing together. When Charles R. Parsons asked Müller if he prayed much, he answered, "Hours every day. But I live in the spirit of prayer; I pray as I walk, when I lie down, and when I rise. And the answers are always coming. Tens of thousands of times my prayers have been answered. When once I am persuaded a thing is right, I go on praying for it until the end comes. I never give up!"[4]

This is important advice for us to remember, surrounded as we are by a dizzying array of prayer books and types, methods, and formulas of prayer. It is not so much the method and frequency of prayer that is the point, but rather living in the spirit of prayer. Jesus emphasized that the only thing that really matters is the desire of our hearts for open communication with God, whether we are praying as individuals or in the body of the Church. That is why simplicity in prayer is best. We also know that we are not in this alone; the Holy Spirit helps us talk with God: "Likewise the Spirit helps us in our weakness; for we do not know how to pray as we ought, but that very Spirit intercedes with sighs too deep for words" (Rom 8:26).

*Can you describe a time you received an unexpected answer to prayer, as George Müller did?*

**REFLECTION QUESTION** Again, allow each member a few moments to answer this question.

This concludes our look at prayer. In the next chapter we will turn our attention to another avenue of communicating with God—the Bible. The Word of God, the record we have of the way God was and is with his people throughout history, is God's primary method of communication with humankind. It informs all of our other communication with him.

After everyone has had a chance to respond, the leader reads this paragraph.

## CLOSING PRAYER

To you, O LORD, I lift up my soul.
Make me to know your ways, O LORD;
    teach me your paths.
Lead me in your truth, and teach me,
    for you are the God of my salvation,
    for you I wait all day long.
"Come," my heart says, "seek his face!"
    Your face, LORD, do I seek.
Give ear to my words, O LORD;
    give heed to my sighing.

Allow some time for members to encourage one another to read the Devotional and Scripture Readings and do the exercise in the following chapter before the next meeting. Then invite the members to be silent for a few moments before leading them in reading the Closing Prayer aloud together.

🕊 At the end of the Closing Prayer, the leader asks for a volunteer to lead the next meeting.

Listen to the sound of my cry,
my King and my God,
for to you I pray. Amen. (PSS 25:1, 4–5; 27:8; 5:1–2)

## TAKING IT FURTHER

**ADDITIONAL EXERCISE**

Ask those people in your life who are strong spiritual mentors about their experiences with prayer and what works best for them.

**ADDITIONAL RESOURCES**

Foster, Richard J. *Meditative Prayer.* Downers Grove, IL: InterVarsity, 1983.

Foster, Richard J. *Prayer: Finding the Heart's True Home.* San Francisco: HarperSanFrancisco, 1992.

Grou, Jean-Nicholas. *How to Pray.* Cambridge: James Clarke, 1955.

**ADDITIONAL REFLECTION QUESTIONS**

*Both readings in this chapter focus on simplicity in prayer. In your opinion, what is the simplest kind of prayer? Is there such a thing as a prayer that is too simple?*

*The words of the Lord's Prayer are so familiar to many of us that they can lose meaning and relevance. In* The Message, *Eugene Peterson translates the Lord's Prayer this way: "Our Father in heaven, Reveal who you are. Set the world right; Do what's best—as above, so below. Keep us alive with three square meals. Keep us forgiven with you and forgiving others. Keep us safe from ourselves and the Devil. You're in charge! You can do anything you want! You're ablaze in beauty! Yes. Yes. Yes"[5] How does this version change or refresh how you think about or pray the Lord's Prayer?*

*Take stock of your own prayer life. Do you view prayer as a burden, another task to be crossed off your list? Or perhaps for you prayer is more difficult than simple. Think about the type of prayer you tried this week as part of the exercise and challenge yourself to come up with a new prayer plan or schedule to incorporate in your daily routine.*

# MEETING GOD
# IN SCRIPTURE

**3**

KEY SCRIPTURE: Nehemiah 8:1–4a, 5–9

## DEVOTIONAL READING

INTRODUCTION TO *The Renovaré Spiritual Formation Bible*

The Bible is all about human life "with God." It is about how God has made this "with-God" life possible and will bring it to pass. In fact, the name Immanuel, meaning in Hebrew "God is with us," is the title given to the one and only Redeemer, because it refers to God's everlasting intent for human life—namely, that we should be in every aspect a dwelling place of God. *Indeed, the unity of the Bible is discovered in the development of life "with God" as a reality on earth, centered in the person of Jesus....*

This dynamic, pulsating, with-God life is on nearly every page of the Bible. To the point of redundancy, we hear that *God is with* his people: with Abraham and Moses, with Esther and David, with Isaiah, Jeremiah, Amos, Micah, Haggai, and Malachi, with Mary, Peter, James, and John, with Paul and Barnabas, with Priscilla and Aquila, with Lydia, Timothy, Epaphroditus, and Phoebe, and with a host of others too numerous to name....

God not only originated the Bible through human authorship; he remains with it always. It is God's book. No one owns it but God himself. It is the loving heart of God made visible and plain. And receiving this message of exquisite love is the great privilege of all who long for life with God. *Reading, studying, memorizing, and meditating upon Scripture have always been the foundation of the Christian disciplines....* And the Bible has been given to help us. God has so superintended the writing of Scripture that it serves as a most reliable guide for our own spiritual formation.[1]

⤴ It is helpful for everyone to read the Devotional and Scripture Readings and do the My Life with God Exercise before the meeting. Begin the meeting with silent prayer, then move directly to Reflecting on My Life with God below.

# MY LIFE WITH GOD EXERCISE

The devotional reading lists four ways to approach Scripture: reading, studying, memorizing, and meditating upon Scripture. We sample each of these approaches in this exercise.

*Reading and Studying.* In the last chapter we cited portions of the Sermon on the Mount and noted how Jesus used the phrase "you have heard that it was said" to point back to the law before teaching something that went beyond what it required. These Scriptures show that Jesus taught that the heart is the source of all our actions and that the condition of the heart has more to do with how we act than do the external laws that we impose on ourselves and try to follow. Keeping in mind this teaching, as well as the quotation from the apostle Paul—"The Law served . . . as our trainer—our guardian, our guide to Christ, to lead us— until [Christ] came" (Gal 3:24, Amplified Bible)—read Exodus 20–40 and Matthew 5–7. As you are reading, listen to what God may be telling you about the relationship between the law and Jesus's teaching.

Here is one way to do the exercise: while you are reading Exodus, write down the regulations you find. Then, as you read the Sermon on the Mount, write down the teachings of Jesus that correspond to the laws in Exodus. There won't be a one-to-one match—in fact, none of them may match exactly. Here is a schedule to help you get organized:

Day 1: Exodus 20–22 and Matthew 5:1–26
Day 2: Exodus 23–26 and Matthew 5:27–48
Day 3: Exodus 27–29 and Matthew 6:1–18
Day 4: Exodus 30–33 and Matthew 6:19–34
Day 5: Exodus 34–37 and Matthew 7:1–14
Day 6: Exodus 38–40 and Matthew 7:15–29

Feel free to try other ways of reading and studying these Scriptures if this schedule doesn't work for you. For example, read everything for six days in a row. Or read all of Exodus before reading the excerpt from Matthew. There is no one way that fits everyone, so do whatever works best for you.

*Meditating and Memorizing.* We encourage you to pick one verse a day from your reading to meditate on for at least fifteen minutes. Try the practice of *lectio divina,* or holy reading. Howard Macy offers some helpful advice for beginning this practice: "Usually it helps to begin 'holy reading' with silence, partly to quiet ourselves to listen and partly to consciously choose to read in a way much different from the other reading we do.

Then we can read, proceeding prayerfully, ready to stop, to soak in a word or a verse as God opens it to us, to brood gently over it, to take it in slowly like a mint melting in the mouth. This kind of reading invites God to teach us in direct and transforming ways."[2] Finally, seek to memorize one or more of the verses on which you meditated. As you read, study, meditate, and memorize, ask the Holy Spirit to heighten your understanding of how the written Word of God shapes your spirit.

*Which aspects of Scripture study were easiest and which were most difficult for you—reading, studying, meditating, or memorizing? Was it helpful to use several different methods of learning the text? Why or why not? As you worked your way through the two passages, did you have a sense that God was speaking to you?*

REFLECTING ON MY LIFE WITH GOD
Allow each member a few moments to answer this question.

## ► SCRIPTURE READING: NEHEMIAH 8:1–4A, 5–9

☞ After everyone has had a chance to respond to the question, ask a member to read this passage from Scripture.

When the seventh month came—the people of Israel being settled in their towns—all the people gathered together into the square before the Water Gate. They told the scribe Ezra to bring the book of the law of Moses, which the LORD had given to Israel. Accordingly, the priest Ezra brought the law before the assembly, both men and women and all who could hear with understanding. This was on the first day of the seventh month. He read from it facing the square before the Water Gate from early morning until midday, in the presence of the men and the women and those who could understand; and the ears of all the people were attentive to the book of the law. The scribe Ezra stood on a wooden platform that had been made for the purpose. . . . And Ezra opened the book in the sight of all the people, for he was standing above all the people; and when he opened it, all the people stood up. Then Ezra blessed the LORD, the great God, and all the people answered, "Amen, Amen," lifting up their hands. Then they bowed their heads and worshiped the LORD with their faces to the ground. Also . . . the Levites helped the people to understand the law, while the people remained in their places. So they read from the book, from the law of God, with interpretation. They gave the sense, so that the people understood the reading.

And Nehemiah, who was the governor, and Ezra the priest and scribe, and the Levites who taught the people said to all the people, "This day is holy to the LORD your God; do not mourn or weep." For all the people wept when they heard the words of the law.

2:7 — Rev 21
Mt 6     Ps 2   Hebrews

**REFLECTION QUESTION**
Allow each person a few
moments to respond to
this question.

*Have you had an experience in which the reading of Scripture (in private study or aloud in a public forum) evoked strong emotions in you?*

## ▶▶ GETTING THE PICTURE

✍ After a brief discus-
sion, choose one person
to read this section.

In this Scripture, the Hebrew people have returned to Jerusalem and Judah after generations of captivity. Among their number are priests, Levites, and temple servants, and in their possession are the Temple utensils taken to Babylon by Nebuchadnezzar, but the people themselves have lost touch with their religious traditions. They no longer know how to live as a holy people. Their leaders, Ezra the priest and Nehemiah the governor, address this problem first by making plans to rebuild the Temple. Once the people are established in their towns, the Israelites lay the foundation for the Temple and, despite opposition from the other inhabitants of the land, reconstruct it as best they can. There Ezra, who "had set his heart to study the law of the LORD," serves as priest and reads the law to the people from a wooden platform specially built for that purpose (Ezra 7:10; Neh 8:4).

Before Ezra reads the law, the people worship, and Levites help the people understand the law as he reads. At the end of the reading, Nehemiah, Ezra, and the Levites tell the people, "This day is holy to the LORD your God; do not mourn or weep," because "all the people wept *when they heard the words of the law*" (Neh 8:9b, emphasis added). Presumably they wept because upon hearing the law they realized how greatly they had failed to keep it. This reading of the law is a watershed moment in Israel's history. Fresh from exile, the people needed to be re-minded of how to live as the People of God, and the law, the Scripture, was the means for doing that. From then on, the Israelites were known as the "People of the Book."

## ▶▶▶ GOING DEEPER

✍ Have another mem-
ber read this section.

We notice several things in this passage. First, reading Scripture was a vital part of worship in the restored Temple. It was the primary way for the people to pass on the traditions associated with the Mosaic law, to hear how God wanted them to live, to listen to his promises. Reading from the Torah was also central to the order of worship in synagogues in the first century. Jesus stood and read aloud from Isaiah in the synagogue in Nazareth when he visited his hometown at the beginning of his ministry (Luke 4:16–20). Similarly, readings from the Bible are still a central element of worship in Christian churches.

We also notice that Ezra's reading from the law had a profound effect on the listeners. Words have power. And it was through the written Word of God that the Israelites learned who God was and who they were. Even today, the living, active, written Word of God has the power to form our spirits because it is "sharper than any two-edged sword, piercing until it divides soul from spirit, joints from marrow; it is able to judge the thoughts and intentions of the heart" (Heb 4:12).

Another fact now becomes apparent: the written Word of God is to be respected. The people stood as Ezra read the Scriptures. Jesus, too, stood as he read the passage from Isaiah in the Nazareth synagogue, as do many Christians today.

Finally, the Scriptures have staying power. They were relevant to the lives of the people after Moses received the law, when the Hebrews returned to Jerusalem after the Exile, while Jesus walked the earth, today, and during all of the centuries in between. The passage makes clear that people knew they were hearing from God when the Scriptures were read and studied. This understanding is highlighted in a letter the apostle Paul wrote to his protégé Timothy to advise him on pastoring the wayward church in Ephesus: "But as for you, continue in what you have learned and firmly believed, knowing from whom you learned it, and how from childhood you have known the sacred writings that are able to instruct you for salvation through faith in Christ Jesus. All scripture is inspired by God and is useful for teaching, for reproof, for correction, and for training in righteousness, so that everyone who belongs to God may be proficient, equipped for every good work" (2 Tim 3:14–17).

*Many of us love to read. There is something very relaxing and enjoyable about curling up with a novel, a newspaper, or a magazine. Yet we don't always have that kind of feeling when we approach spending time reading the Bible. If this is the case for you, why is this true? What might be done to change this?*

**REFLECTION QUESTION**
Allow each person a few moments to respond.

*[handwritten: More- I've done it so much too familiar + not innovative enough.]*

>>>> **POINTING TO GOD**

The people to whom Ezra read wept when they heard the powerful words of Scripture. Indeed, countless Christians—including one of

Choose one member to read this section.

Christianity's greatest and most influential thinkers, Augustine—have found faith simply by reading Scripture. As a young man, Augustine read the Bible with his friend Alypius and was overcome by his own sinfulness. He left his friend and wept, pleading with God to forgive him. Then he heard a child's voice chanting from a neighboring yard, "Pick it up, read it; pick it up, read it." Not being able to recall any child's song with such a peculiar verse, he wondered if it might be a message from God. He picked up a Bible and opened it at random to read, "Not in rioting and in drunkenness, not in chambering and wantonness, not in strife and envying, but put on the Lord Jesus Christ, and make no provision for the flesh to fulfill the lusts thereof" (Rom 13:13–14).

Many years later, Augustine wrote about the experience in his *Confessions*:

> I wanted to read no further, nor did I need to. For instantly, as the sentence ended, there was infused in my heart something like the light of full certainty and all the gloom of doubt vanished away. Closing the book, then, and putting my finger or something else for a mark I began—now with a tranquil countenance—to tell it all to Alypius. And he in turn disclosed to me what had been going on in himself, of which I knew nothing. He asked to see what I had read. I showed him, and he looked on even further than I had read. I had not known what followed. But indeed it was this, "Him that is weak in the faith, receive." This he applied to himself, and told me so. By these words of warning he was strengthened, and by exercising his good resolution and purpose—all very much in keeping with his character, in which, in these respects, he was always far different from and better than I—he joined me in full commitment without any restless hesitation.[3]

Augustine was not unfamiliar with Christianity or with the Bible before that day in the garden. But on this occasion he no longer looked at the Bible from an abstract, intellectual point of view but regarded it as a living document that could be understood in terms of his own experience, in relation to *him*. We too must remember that all the people whose experiences are described in the Bible are mere humans, just like us. To profit fully from the teaching of Scripture, it is right and good—perhaps even essential—to put ourselves in their shoes, to seek to understand their thoughts and emotions. It is the only way we can open ourselves to experiences of God similar to theirs! Think of Augustine's story and those of countless others who became believers just by reading the written Word of God. If God can use the Bible to reach those who are not yet believers, just think what lessons he can teach those of us who approach the Bible with an open and eager heart, ready to meet him.

## ▶▶▶▶▶ GOING FORWARD

The Bible is God's gift to us, to be used in worship, study, and meditation to learn more about him and to become as much like him as we can. For many Christians, our greatest failure is failing to read and study the Bible enough, or even at all. But there are also dangers that we must consider when studying the Bible. Like Augustine before he heard the voice chanting, "Pick it up, read it," we sometimes approach the Bible solely on an analytical level, rather than as a means to learn about and encounter God. As discussed earlier, one key to avoiding this pitfall is to relate the Bible to our own experiences. *Application*

Conversely, it is possible to take this too far and experience the Bible only on our own, without the help of the Holy Spirit. In Bible study, we should always focus on listening to God, not on confirming our own biases. An extreme example is the way slave owners cited the Bible as support for their practices. It is possible to find an isolated phrase or sentence in the Bible to buttress just about any argument, but reading the Bible this way does not help in spiritual formation. We always must ask God to help us understand.

A final danger is worship of the Bible itself—"bibliolatry" or what Dallas Willard calls "Bible deism,"[4] putting the Bible ahead of God, Jesus Christ, and the Holy Spirit. Although the Bible is a manifestation of God's Word, it is only *one* of them. Jesus Christ was, of course, the living manifestation of the Word. The Bible is only an avenue to God, not God himself. But it remains, as we read in the Devotional Reading, "a most reliable guide for our own spiritual formation." *Going to India*

*When has God spoken directly to you through Scripture?*

This concludes our look at meeting God in Scripture. In the next chapter we will turn our attention to another avenue of communicating with God—listening to God through the creation.

*# of Versions/ translations*

✍ Have another person read this section.

**REFLECTION QUESTION**
Again, allow each member a few moments to answer this question.

✍ After everyone has had a chance to respond, the leader reads this paragraph.

✒ **Allow some time for members to encourage one another to read the Devotional and Scripture Readings and do the exercise in the following chapter before the next meeting.** Then invite the members to be silent for a few moments before leading them in reading the Closing Prayer aloud together.

✒ At the end of the Closing Prayer, the leader asks for a volunteer to lead the next meeting.

# CLOSING PRAYER

To you, O LORD, I lift up my soul.
Make me to know your ways, O LORD;
    teach me your paths.
Lead me in your truth, and teach me,
    for you are the God of my salvation,
    for you I wait all day long.
"Come," my heart says, "seek his face!"
    Your face, LORD, do I seek.
Give ear to my words, O LORD;
    give heed to my sighing.
Listen to the sound of my cry,
    my King and my God,
    for to you I pray. Amen. (PSS 25:1, 4–5; 27:8; 5:1–2)

## TAKING IT FURTHER

**ADDITIONAL EXERCISE**

Attend a service at a Jewish synagogue in your community. Pay special attention to the way they present and celebrate the reading of the Torah. What lessons can you learn about the role of Scripture?

**ADDITIONAL RESOURCES**

Fee, Gordon D., and Douglas Stuart. *How to Read the Bible for All It's Worth.* Grand Rapids, MI: Zondervan, 1982.

Foster, Richard J., and others, eds. *The Renovaré Spiritual Formation Bible.* San Francisco: HarperSanFrancisco, 2005.

Howard, Evan. *Praying the Scriptures: A Field Guide for Your Spiritual Journey.* Downers Grove, IL: InterVarsity, 1999.

**ADDITIONAL REFLECTION QUESTIONS**

*In the passage from Nehemiah, the Levites helped the others understand the Scripture. Who or what fulfills that role in your life?*

*Do you tend to study the Bible more as an individual or in a group setting? What are the advantages or disadvantages of each? Why are both important?*

*In the passage from Nehemiah, the people stood when the Scripture was read. Do modern churches show similar respect for the written Word of God? What are some appropriate ways to show respect for the Bible?*

# LISTENING TO GOD THROUGH THE CREATION

**4**

**KEY SCRIPTURE: Job 9:4–10**

## DEVOTIONAL READING

ST. FRANCIS OF ASSISI, *Francis and Clare: The Complete Writings*

### *The Canticle of Brother Sun*

Most High, all-powerful, good Lord,
Yours are the praises, the glory, the honor, and all blessing.
To You alone, Most High, do they belong,
     and no man is worthy to mention Your name.
Praised be You, my Lord, with all your creatures,
     especially Sir Brother Sun,
Who is the day and through whom You give us light.
And he is beautiful and radiant with great splendor;
     and bears a likeness of You, Most High One.
Praised be You, my Lord, through Sister Moon and the stars,
     in heaven You formed them clear and precious and
          beautiful.
Praised be You, my Lord, through Brother Wind,
     and through the air, cloudy and serene, and every kind
          of weather
     through which You give sustenance to Your creatures.
Praised be You, my Lord, through Sister Water,
     which is very useful and humble and precious and chaste.
Praised be You, my Lord, through Brother Fire,
     through whom You light the night
     and he is beautiful and playful and robust and strong.
Praised be You, my Lord, through our Sister Mother Earth,
     who sustains and governs us,

*[handwritten annotations: "see / feel / smell / hear" near "light"; "constant / a hint" near "Moon and the stars"; "blows away / & carries along" near "Brother Wind"; "The base of all things living" near "Sister Water / Brother Fire"]*

It is helpful for everyone to read the Devotional and Scripture Readings and do the My Life with God Exercise before the meeting. Begin the meeting with silent prayer, then move directly to Reflecting on My Life with God below.

*to nourish body + delight eyes*

and who produces varied fruits with colored flowers and
    herbs.
Praised be you, My Lord, through those who give pardon for
    Your love
and bear infirmity and tribulation.
Blessed are those who endure in peace
    for by You, Most High, they shall be crowned.
Praised be You, my Lord, through our Sister Bodily Death,
    from whom no living man can escape.
Woe to those who die in mortal sin.
Blessed are those whom death will find in Your most holy will,
    for the second death shall do them no harm.
Praise and bless my Lord and give Him thanks
    and serve Him with great humility.[1]

## MY LIFE WITH GOD EXERCISE

Francis of Assisi was known for his ability to see and hear God in the
creation around him. In this exercise we too will tune ourselves to the
language of the universe. Start by reading "The Canticle of Brother Sun"
and Job 9:4–10. Jot down the parts of nature that are mentioned and
reflect on them. You may want to separate them into categories: things
you can touch, such as water and flowers; things you can see, such as
sun and color; and things you can feel, such as wind and heat. You could
even photocopy the texts and mark the categories in different colors.

Next, go for a walk and list things you notice that aren't mentioned
in either reading—sounds, shadows, and so on. Don't be concerned
about listening for God through the creation at this point. Just concen-
trate on observing and praying that God may show you other ways he is
trying to communicate with you through the creation.

On your next walk, prayerfully take your two lists with you and
focus on listening to what God may say to you through such things as
colors, the sounds you hear, the animals you encounter, the people you
meet, the feel of the wind on your face, or the play of shadows on the
landscape. You may want to start by praising God for all of the things
you see around you, as Francis did in his canticle. Or focus on one
aspect each day—things you feel, things you see, things you touch or
smell. Once you get the idea, you'll find that God uses numerous things
in the creation to speak to you. Don't get discouraged if you find this

exercise hard at first. Just because we have trouble hearing does not mean that God isn't speaking to us. Sometimes it takes a lifetime to hear what God is saying to us through the creation, his written Word, and the Holy Spirit.

*What was the most surprising thing you found God in? What else did you learn and discover on your walks?*

**REFLECTING ON MY LIFE WITH GOD**
Allow each member a few moments to answer this question.

➤ **SCRIPTURE READING:** JOB 9:4–10

*God is in all the "natural" working of earth*

> [God] is wise in heart, and mighty in strength
> —who has resisted him, and succeeded?—
> he who removes mountains, and they do not know it,
> when he overturns them in his anger;
> who shakes the earth out of its place,
> and its pillars tremble;
> who commands the sun, and it does not rise;
> who seals up the stars;
> who alone stretched out the heavens
> and trampled the waves of the Sea;
> who made the Bear and Orion,
> the Pleiades and the chambers of the south;
> who does great things beyond understanding,
> and marvelous things without number.

*God is the creator & the controller of His creation*

After everyone has had a chance to respond to the question, ask a member to read this passage from Scripture.

*If you could use only one word to describe the God in the passage above, what would it be? Why?* Commander

**REFLECTION QUESTION**
Allow each person a few moments to respond to this question.

➤➤ **GETTING THE PICTURE**

The book of Job is the story of a wealthy man who loses almost everything—children, possessions, and health—in a test allowed by God to prove that he would remain faithful to God. During his suffering, three people whom Job considers friends sit with him for seven days, at the end of which Job curses the day he was born (3:1–26). His friends respond by lecturing him. Eliphaz contends that Job has sinned. Job replies that his complaint against God is just and explains his reasons.

After a brief discussion, choose one person to read this section.

*Listening to God Through the Creation*                                    35

Bildad tells Job that he should repent and God will "fill [Job's] mouth with laughter, and [his] lips with shouts of joy" (8:21). Job responds, "Indeed I know that this is so; but how can a mortal be just before God? If one wished to contend with him, one could not answer him once in a thousand" (9:2–3). The Scripture Reading gives the rest of Job's answer as he looks to the creation for what it teaches about God's nature and character.

## ▶▶▶ GOING DEEPER

🕊 Have another member read this section.

When we read Job's words, we must remember that he was in pain. Job had seen just about everything he held dear taken away from him, seemingly without reason. Everything he saw was filtered through this veil of pain and suffering. Yet even his anguished words show us fundamental realities about the creation and what it teaches us about God, realities supported by Scripture and devotional writings like "The Canticle of Brother Sun." We see that the Lord is the Creator of the heavens and the earth and of all living things and natural phenomena. We are first taught this in Genesis: "God saw everything that he had made, and indeed, it was very good. And there was evening and there was morning, the sixth day. Thus the heavens and the earth were finished, and all their multitude" (Gen 1:31–2:1). These verses set in motion the story of the earth and the history of mankind, which continue today. Job knew that God created the heavens and the earth; the evidence was all around him. The mountains, the earth, the sun, and the heavens all attested to the fact that they had been made by the same Creator. Yet whereas Francis exulted in the beauty of the creation, its very magnificence made Job feel small. He wanted to argue with God, to plead his case as he would before an earthly judge, but he felt too small and insignificant to do so before one who is so powerful, one who "does great things beyond understanding, and marvelous things without number."

We also learn that God's action in creation continues. For Job, God overturned mountains in his anger. The earth shook. Lost in undeserved suffering, Job was frightened by God's continuing action in creation, which shows God's power and our powerlessness. But in "The Canticle of Brother Sun," Francis shows us that God's action in creation is also sustaining and nurturing. God gives us weather to sustain us and fire to light our way in the night. We can only conclude that if God continues to act within his creation, we should pay attention to what he is doing.

CONNECTING WITH GOD

Finally, even though inexplicably tragic disasters, including hurricanes, tornadoes, tsunamis, and earthquakes, may shake our lives and make us wonder if God has abandoned the earth, if we step back and look at the big picture, we see that the earth is an orderly place. Although we, like Job, know that things happen that we do not understand, there are other things that we can depend on. The sun continues to give us light for each day, and the moon follows its twenty-eight-day cycle. After a huge earthquake, the earth may ring like a bell for a few hours, but it stays on its axis and continues to rotate so that we have day and night, and continues to go around the sun every year, which gives us seasons. This orderliness assures us that God is still in control, an assurance echoed in "The Canticle of Brother Sun" as it depicts God sustaining humankind with weather, water to quench people's thirst, and food to sate their appetites. *and the march to death –*

REFLECTION QUESTION
Allow each person a few moments to respond.

*The Devotional Reading and the passage from Job show us that God is in charge of the creation. How do you react to this teaching? Do you find it a cause for celebration, as Francis does, or do you, like Job, find it a little disturbing? Why?*

*As time goes on, I am more convinced / conulcted that all occurrences, be it tornado or a rainbow, are con purposed. He either stays his hand or lets it loose*

### ▶▶▶ POINTING TO GOD *but all for a purpose*

As we saw in the Devotional Reading, St. Francis of Assisi, an Italian mystic of the thirteenth century, saw God in all living things. In *The Little Flowers of St. Francis of Assisi*, the story of how he preached to the birds gives us insight into the way Francis experienced and understood God through the creation:

Choose one member to read this section.

> And as he went on his way, with great fervour, St Francis lifted up his eyes, and saw on some trees by the wayside a great multitude of birds; and being much surprised, he said to his companions, "Wait for me here by the way, whilst I go and preach to my little sisters the birds"; and entering into the field, he began to preach to the birds. . . . Now the substance of the sermon was this: "My little sisters the birds, ye owe much to God, your Creator, and ye ought to sing his praise at all times and in all places, because he has given you liberty to fly about into all places; and though ye neither spin nor sew, he has given you a twofold and a threefold clothing for yourselves and for your offspring. Two of all your species he sent into the Ark with [Noah] that you might not be lost

to the world; besides which, he feeds you, though ye neither sow nor reap. He has given you fountains and rivers to quench your thirst, mountains and valleys in which to take refuge, and trees in which to build your nests; so that your Creator loves you much, having thus favoured you with such bounties. Beware, my little sisters, of the sin of ingratitude, and study always to give praise to God." As he said these words, all the birds began to open their beaks, to stretch their necks, to spread their wings and reverently to bow their heads to the ground, endeavouring by their motions and by their songs to manifest their joy to St Francis. And the saint rejoiced with them. He wondered to see such a multitude of birds, and was charmed with their beautiful variety, with their attention and familiarity, for all which he devoutly gave thanks to the Creator. Having finished his sermon, St Francis made the sign of the cross, and gave them leave to fly away. Then all those birds rose up into the air, singing most sweetly; and, following the sign of the cross, which St Francis had made, they divided themselves into four companies. One company flew towards the east, another towards the west, one towards the south, and one towards the north; each company as it went singing most wonderfully; signifying thereby, that … the humble friars, like little birds, should possess nothing in this world, but should cast all the care of their lives on the providence of God.[2]

We don't know if this story happened exactly as it is described here, but in any case we can learn from Francis's attitude toward the creation. Francis stops his journey to do a rather strange and astonishing thing: preach to the birds. The point is not so much that we should be evangelizing wildlife but rather that we can and should pay attention to God's beautiful creation. Francis tells the birds that they owe much to God for creating them, caring for them, and giving them natural resources to shelter, water, and feed them. Therefore they should be grateful and praise him. As Francis enumerates everything he has noticed about the birds and their condition, we humans can't help but notice that God has given us all the same blessings and more. How well God cares for us. We too should praise him! Francis delights in seeing the birds, their graceful motions, their cheerful songs, and their beautiful color and variety. This joy he experiences in the creation is a twofold lesson for us. Not only should we delight in the beauty of the creation around us, but we can experience this joy as a small taste of the joy God finds in us.

We know that God created this world and is in charge of it. Furthermore, he is still present in the creation. It's important to look for God's presence in all living things. Not only does it help us to learn more about the nature of God but also, as Francis's sermon demonstrates, we learn to accept and celebrate our dependence on God, which in turn teaches us humility. As Francis shows us, we can delight in the beauty and order of what God has created. This, too, is a form of communicating with God. Whenever we're gardening, hiking, enjoying a sunset, or smelling or admiring a flower, we can offer a thankful prayer to God. We can open ourselves to the lessons God has to teach with each piece of the creation and appreciate how beautifully each interlocking piece serves his ends.

> *Have another person read this section.*

We must remember, however, that although God is present *in* the creation to sustain it and to keep chaos at bay, the creation is *not* God. Paul writes that "all things hold together" in or by Christ (Col 1:17b), but neither God the Father nor the Son nor the Holy Spirit *is* the creation. We worship the Creator, not the creation. This is a tension we must keep in mind as we listen to God through such things as the beauty of a sunset, the fragrance of a flower, the flavor of salt, the song of a bird, the wetness of water.

*Francis taught us a lesson about God through the birds. Through what animal or other part of the creation have you learned a lesson about God? What are some other ways in which you could learn about God through the creation?*

> **REFLECTION QUESTION**
> Again, allow each member a few moments to answer this question.

This concludes our look at listening to God through the creation. In the next chapter we will turn our attention to another avenue of communicating with God—hearing God through other people.

> *After everyone has had a chance to respond, the leader reads this paragraph.*

> *Allow some time for members to encourage one another to read the Devotional and Scripture Readings and do the exercise in the following chapter before the next meeting.* Then invite the members to be silent for a few moments before leading them in reading the Closing Prayer aloud together.

## CLOSING PRAYER

To you, O LORD, I lift up my soul.
Make me to know your ways, O LORD;
        teach me your paths.
Lead me in your truth, and teach me,
        for you are the God of my salvation,
        for you I wait all day long.
"Come," my heart says, "seek his face!"
        Your face, LORD, do I seek.

At the end of the Closing Prayer, the leader asks for a volunteer to lead the next meeting.

Give ear to my words, O Lᴏʀᴅ;
  give heed to my sighing.
Listen to the sound of my cry,
  my King and my God,
    for to you I pray. Amen. (ᴘss 25:1, 4–5; 27:8; 5:1–2)

## TAKING IT FURTHER

**ADDITIONAL EXERCISE**

Take a few minutes to sit outside in a beautiful place and do what Francis of Assisi did: delight in the beauty and variety of nature. Think about how God cares for the plants and the animals you see and how well planned and complex his creation is. Bring your Bible if you like and read Psalm 19:1–6.

**ADDITIONAL RESOURCES**

di Monte Santa Maria, Brother Ugolino. *The Little Flowers of St. Francis.* Trans. Raphael Brown. New York: Doubleday/Image, 1958.
Foster, Richard J., and others, eds. *The Renovaré Spiritual Formation Bible.* San Francisco: HarperSanFrancisco, 2005.

**ADDITIONAL REFLECTION QUESTIONS**

*What else does studying and thinking about the creation tell you about God and the way he relates to us?*

*Francis of Assisi addressed the sun, moon, stars, and animals as "brother" and "sister." How do you react to this? What does this say to you about our role within the creation?*

*In what other ways do you see God continuing to work through the creation?*

# HEARING GOD THROUGH OTHER PEOPLE

## 5

**KEY SCRIPTURE: 2 Samuel 12:1–10a, 11a, 13–14**

## DEVOTIONAL READING

DALLAS WILLARD, *Hearing God*

No means of communication between God and us is more commonly used in the Bible or the history of the church than the voice of a definite, individual human being. In such cases God and the person he uses speak *conjointly*. It may be that the one spoken *to* is also the one spoken *through*.... [T]he word is at once the word of God, God's message, and the word of the human being who is also speaking.

The two do not exclude each other any more than humanity and divinity exclude each other in the person of Jesus Christ. We can say that God speaks through us, as long as this is not understood as automatically ruling out *our* speaking *with* God and even, in an important sense, *through* God. The relationship must *not* be understood as an essentially mechanical one with God simply using us as we might use a telephone. No doubt that would be God's option should he choose, but usually he does not....

I believe I can say with assurance that God's speaking in union with the human voice and human language is the primary *objective* way in which God addresses us. That is, of all the ways in which a message comes from *outside* the mind or personality of the person addressed, it most commonly comes through a human being.

This is best suited to the purposes of God precisely because it *most fully engages the faculties of free, intelligent beings who are socially interacting with agape love in the work of God as his colaborers and friends.* This is obvious from the contents of the Bible. And of course the Bible is itself a case of God's speaking along with human beings—usually so in the process of its delivery to humankind and now always as it continues to speak to us today.[1]

It is helpful for everyone to read the Devotional and Scripture Readings and do the My Life with God Exercise before the meeting. Begin the meeting with silent prayer, then move directly to Reflecting on My Life with God below.

# MY LIFE WITH GOD EXERCISE

In the Devotional Reading, Dallas Willard notes that sometimes "the one spoken *to* is also the one spoken *through*." This is illustrated by the Scripture chosen for the reading, which describes the Lord sending the prophet Nathan—the one spoken *to* and *through*—to speak to David about his sin. Like the word given to Nathan, a word from God may be given to a person we know well or even a stranger as a way to correct our behavior or identify a wrong we have committed. At other times, the word that comes through an intermediary guides, encourages, warns, or enlightens us. Many of us have never been aware of receiving a direct word from God that we then pass on to another person, but some of us have at times heard a word through a teacher, minister, or priest in the form of a sermon, devotional, lecture, or lesson that was especially applicable to a particular situation we faced.

For the next few days, read the excerpt from *Hearing God* at least once a day. As you read, let its truths sink deep into your heart. Then, as you go about your daily routine—there's no need to do anything special—be aware of advice you receive from others, offhand comments they may make about your work or you as an individual, and conversations you may have with people on the telephone, while shopping, or during breaks. When you go to church functions, pay careful attention to what the leaders teach and preach. As you listen to others, be quietly attentive to the Lord and ask, "What are you trying to tell me?" You may want to carry a small piece of paper or a notebook to write down impressions about what God may be saying to you through other people. If you have never done this before, it may be a little hard at the beginning. But as you become more accustomed to listening for the voice of God through other people, it will become easier.

**REFLECTING ON MY LIFE WITH GOD**
Allow each member a few moments to answer this question.

*What did you find most difficult about listening for the voice of God through other people? The easiest? Without naming names, who were some of the people who had a word from God for you? Describe any "aha!" experiences—something you had been thinking or feeling but hadn't been able to put into words, or something in which you needed guidance but had been afraid or hesitant to ask.*

⨿ After everyone has had a chance to respond to the question, ask a member to read this passage from Scripture.

▶ **SCRIPTURE READING:** 2 SAMUEL 12:1–10A, 11A, 13–14

But the thing that David had done displeased the LORD, and the LORD sent Nathan to David. He came to him and said to him, "There were two men in a certain city, the one rich and the other poor. The rich man had very many flocks and herds; but the poor man had nothing but one little ewe lamb, which he had bought. He brought it up, and it grew up with him and with his children; it used to eat of his meager fare, and drink from his cup, and lie in his bosom, and it was like a daughter to him. Now there came a traveler to the rich man, and he was loath to take one of his own flock or herd to prepare for the wayfarer who had come to him, but he took the poor man's lamb, and prepared that for the guest who had come to him." Then David's anger was greatly kindled against the man. He said to Nathan, "As the LORD lives, the man who has done this deserves to die; he shall restore the lamb fourfold, because he did this thing, and because he had no pity."

Nathan said to David, "You are the man! Thus says the LORD, the God of Israel: I anointed you king over Israel, and I rescued you from the hand of Saul; I gave you your master's house, and your master's wives into your bosom, and gave you the house of Israel and of Judah; and if that had been too little, I would have added as much more. Why have you despised the word of the LORD, to do what is evil in his sight? You have struck down Uriah the Hittite with the sword, and have taken his wife to be your wife, and have killed him with the sword of the Ammonites. Now therefore the sword shall never depart from your house.... Thus says the LORD: I will raise up trouble against you from within your own house...." David said to Nathan, "I have sinned against the LORD." Nathan said to David, "Now the LORD has put away your sin; you shall not die. Nevertheless, because by this deed you have utterly scorned the LORD, the child that is born to you shall die."

*Reflect on your personal experience. Have you ever been told by another person that your behavior was wrong or told another person that he or she had behaved badly? If so, how did you feel? How do you think Nathan felt about having to tell David that his actions were sinful? How would you react if you were David?*

**REFLECTION QUESTION**
Allow each person a few moments to respond to this question.

## ►► GETTING THE PICTURE

To get a sense of how uncharacteristic David's sin is, we need to backtrack a little. David, the youngest of Jesse's eight sons, is anointed by the prophet Samuel as king of the nation of Israel while Saul is still on the throne, and "the spirit of the LORD came mightily upon David from that day forward" (1 Sam 16:13b). When the spirit of the LORD leaves

🖎 After a brief discussion, choose one person to read this section.

Saul, Saul engages David's services as a lyre player. During his service to Saul, David slays the giant Goliath in a battle with the Philistines, which inspires the Hebrews to chant "Saul has killed his thousands, and David his ten thousands" as they celebrate Saul's victory over the Philistines (18:7b). This sends Saul into such a jealous rage that he twice tries to kill David. In an attempt to get rid of him, Saul promises his daughter Michal to David, with one provision: that he cut off the foreskins of a hundred Philistines. David is successful, and "Saul gave him his daughter Michal as a wife" (18:27). When "Saul realized that the LORD was with David" and that Michal loves him, he becomes more afraid of David and considers him an enemy (18:28–29).

Because of Saul's anger, David has to leave Jerusalem. He becomes widely known after avoiding capture by Saul's men for several years. Although he fears for his life at Saul's hand, David mourns when Saul and his sons—including Jonathan, who "loved [David] as his own soul"—are killed in another battle with the Philistines (18:1c; 31:1–6; 2 Sam 1–12). After being instructed by the LORD to go to Hebron in Judah, David settles there with his two wives. In Hebron the people anoint him "king over the house of Judah" (2 Sam 2:4). Upon his ascension to the throne, David begins consolidating his power. He wins wars, becoming king over all Israel, and moves to Jerusalem (the capital of the united kingdom), bringing the Ark of the Covenant. At the height of his power and influence, David sees Bathsheba, the wife of Uriah the Hittite, taking a bath and covets her. The account in 2 Samuel simply records, "So David sent messengers to get her, and she came to him, and he lay with her.... The woman conceived; and she sent and told David, 'I am pregnant'" (11:4–5). To cover his tracks, David conspires to bring Uriah, a soldier, back to Jerusalem so that he can have sexual intercourse with his wife, but Uriah refuses to leave the troops. So David orders his general, Joab, to send Uriah to the front lines so that he will be killed at the siege of Rabbah. Then David brings Bathsheba into his house as his wife. At this point Nathan confronts David with his sin.

### ▶▶▶ GOING DEEPER

*Have another member read this section.*

As we examine this passage, we first notice that Nathan was sent by God. God spoke *to* Nathan, a specific person, about David's sin, and then spoke *through* Nathan to David. As Dallas Willard states in the Devotional Reading, "The word is at once the word of God, God's message,

CONNECTING WITH GOD

and the word of the human being who is also speaking." Nathan stood in a long line of prophets through which God relayed messages to the Hebrews. Not only did he obey God and deliver the message to David, but Nathan made no attempt to soften God's message, although David could have killed him or had him killed on the spot. Nathan stood his ground and delivered the message as he had been directed by God.

God's word for David came through the living personality, mind, and body of Nathan, who customized it to fit his style of communication. Nathan wisely couched God's message to David in the form of a story. The story let David draw his own conclusion and recommend a punishment for the rich man. Nathan did not accuse David of anything; instead he let David indict himself. Jesus used this method many times in his parables. Sometimes the people understood the meaning of the parables; at other times they did not. When the disciples asked Jesus why he spoke in parables, he answered, "The reason I speak to them in parables is that 'seeing they do not perceive, and hearing they do not listen, nor do they understand' … But blessed are your eyes, for they see, and your ears, for they hear" (Matt 13:13, 16). David heard and understood God's message.

One thing that makes Nathan's story about the rich man's confiscation of the poor man's lamb so compelling is the comparison it draws between rich and poor. Underlying these comparisons is the fact that the rich man had the power to take what he wanted using any methods he wanted, and the poor man was powerless to stop him. Even though David came from a humble background as a shepherd, he had evidently forgotten how precious each sheep is to a person who has very little money. He had lost touch with the common person. God's message was "customized" for David.

Nathan's message from God prompted David to repent, but his sin still had serious consequences. As predicted, David and his descendants knew unending grief. The child born to Bathsheba died. Trouble came into David's household when one son raped a stepsister and another son took revenge and had his stepbrother killed. Later the same son usurped David's throne, forcing David to flee Jerusalem. God's message to David from Nathan prompted David to repent of his sin but could not head off future trouble.

*Did you ever feel that God had given you a message to pass on to someone else? If so, did you honor the feeling? How did you put the message? If you have never had this experience, how do you think such a message might come to you? Do you think you would have the courage to express it?*

**REFLECTION QUESTION**
Allow each person a few moments to respond.

✍ Choose one member to read this section.

The passage we just read describes others speaking to us with an audible voice, but we can also receive God's messages through the writings of others. One example is Sheldon Vanauken. When he and his wife, Davy, went to Oxford to study in the early 1950s, they were not Christians. However, the atmosphere of the college and some close Christian friends encouraged them to look more deeply into the Christian faith. They read numerous theological classics and contemporary works, as well as the New Testament in several translations. But as Vanauken wrote, "There is no doubt that C. S. Lewis was, first to last, overwhelmingly the most important reading for us both. Only someone who has faced the question—is Christianity false?—can help someone else resolve the counter-question—is it true?... [H]e wrote about Christianity in a style as clear as spring water without a hint of sanctimoniousness or vagueness or double-talk, never suggesting that anything be accepted on other than reasonable grounds. He gave us, simply, straightforward, telling argument laced with wit."[2] Just as Nathan's story of the poor man's lamb spoke clearly to David because of his background as a shepherd, so C. S. Lewis's writing especially touched Vanauken and his wife because they were approaching Christianity from an academic point of view. Vanauken in particular was motivated to look more deeply into Christianity because he was impressed by its hold over those he considered brilliant. "If minds like St. Augustine's and Newman's and Lewis's could wrestle with Christianity and become fortresses of that faith, it had to be taken seriously," he wrote.[3]

Vanauken was so stirred by the writings of C. S. Lewis that he started to write him letters. The two struck up a correspondence and a friendship that would endure to the end of Lewis's life. In their first few letters, Vanauken expressed his questions and doubts about Christianity and Lewis answered. In a typical exchange, Vanauken asked why faith was necessary and why God didn't just make his existence clear. Lewis responded:

> I do not think there is a *demonstrative* proof (like Euclid) of Christianity, nor of the existence of matter, nor of the good will & honesty of my best & oldest friends. I think all three are (except perhaps the second) far more probable than the alternatives.... I demand from my friend a trust in my good faith which is *certain* without demonstrative proof. It wouldn't be confidence

at all if he waited for rigorous proof. Hang it all, the very fairy-tales embody the truth. Othello believed in Desdemona's innocence when it was proved: but that was too late. Lear believed in Cordelia's love when it was proved: but that was too late. 'His praise is lost who stays till all commend.' The magnanimity, the generosity [which] will trust on a reasonable probability, is required of us.

Lewis ended the letter, "But I think you are already in the meshes of the net! The Holy Spirit is after you. I doubt if you'll get away!"[4]—a sentiment that alarmed Vanauken, who was not sure at the time that he wanted to be enmeshed in God's net! But when Vanauken and his wife became Christians soon after, they both credited Lewis with helping to show them the way.

## ▶▶▶▶▶ GOING FORWARD

God uses many people to communicate with us—pastors, friends, acquaintances, mentors, spouses, family. It is up to us to cultivate the habit of listening for his words. Sometimes the message is one we enjoy hearing, such as an answer to a question we have, the solution to a problem we are facing, an insight that gives us more faith, a confirmation that we are going in the right direction, or a warning before we make a mistake. At other times, as with Nathan's message to David, the words may be hard to hear but beneficial in the long run. God wants only good for us, and in the course of our lives he will send people who help to bring and keep that good in our lives.

*Have another person read this section.*

Listening to God through others is supernatural and natural at the same time. We just need to listen. Sounds easy, doesn't it? But as with all of the other ways of listening to God, it begs the important question: how do we know when it's God? We should question any message we think we have received if it contradicts what we know about God from the Bible. But we can look other places as well for confirmation of a message from God. Jean Darnell advises confirming any message three ways. "If you believe God has told you to do something, ask him to confirm it to you three times: through his word, through circumstances, and through other people who may know nothing of the situation."[5]

REFLECTION QUESTION
Again, allow each mem-
ber a few moments to
answer this question.

*Who do you think are the prophets in modern-day society? What about in your life?*

🕊 After everyone has
had a chance to respond,
the leader reads this
paragraph.

This concludes our look at hearing God through other people. In the next chapter we will turn our attention to another avenue of communicating with God—perceiving God in circumstances.

🕊 **Allow some time for
members to encourage
one another to read the
Devotional and Scrip-
ture Readings and do
the exercise in the fol-
lowing chapter before
the next meeting.** Then
invite the members to be
silent for a few moments
before leading them
in reading the Closing
Prayer aloud together.

## CLOSING PRAYER

To you, O LORD, I lift up my soul.
Make me to know your ways, O LORD;
    teach me your paths.
Lead me in your truth, and teach me,
    for you are the God of my salvation,
    for you I wait all day long.
"Come," my heart says, "seek his face!"
    Your face, LORD, do I seek.
Give ear to my words, O LORD;
    give heed to my sighing.
Listen to the sound of my cry,
    my King and my God,
    for to you I pray. Amen. (PSS 25:1, 4–5; 27:8; 5:1–2)

🕊 At the end of the
Closing Prayer, the leader
asks for a volunteer to
lead the next meeting.

## TAKING IT FURTHER

Make a list of all or some of the people through whom you believe you have received a message from God. Consider thanking them in person or by a letter. Observe their reactions to see if you can learn something about the way God speaks to them and works through them.

Bonhoeffer, Dietrich. *Letters and Papers from Prison.* New York: Simon & Schuster/ Touchstone, 1971.

Huggett, Joyce. *The Joy of Listening to God.* Downers Grove, IL: InterVarsity, 1986.

Vanauken, Sheldon. *A Severe Mercy.* San Francisco: HarperSanFrancisco, 1977.

Willard, Dallas. *Hearing God,* 3d ed. Downers Grove, IL: InterVarsity, 1999.

*Nathan didn't pull any punches in passing God's message on to David. What do you think might have happened if he had softened the message? How might you pass on a similar message to, say, your best friend?*

*Willard makes it clear in the Devotional Reading that God hardly ever speaks through us mechanically, like we might speak through a telephone. What, then, is the role of the individual when God is speaking through him or her? Could we ignore the impulse or jumble the message?*

*Why do you think God chose Nathan to pass on the message rather than telling David himself?*

# PERCEIVING GOD IN CIRCUMSTANCES

6

KEY SCRIPTURE: Genesis 45:4–15; 50:19–20

## DEVOTIONAL READING

PHILIP YANCEY, *Finding God in Unexpected Places*

The job of a journalist is, simply, to see. We are professional eyes. As a Christian journalist, I have learned to look for traces of God. I have found those traces in unexpected places.... On a trip to South Africa, I met a remarkable woman named Joanna. She is of mixed race, part black and part white, a category known there as "Coloured." As a student she agitated for change in apartheid and then saw the miracle that no one had predicted, the peaceful dismantling of that evil system. Afterward, for many hours she sat with her husband and watched live broadcasts of the Truth and Reconciliation Commission hearings.

Instead of simply exulting in her newfound freedoms, Joanna next decided to tackle the most violent prison in South Africa, a prison where Nelson Mandela had spent several years. Tattoo-covered gang members controlled the prison, strictly enforcing a rule that required new members to earn their admittance to the gang by assaulting undesirable prisoners. Prison authorities looked the other way, letting these "animals" beat and even kill each other.

Alone, this attractive young woman started going each day into the bowels of that prison. She brought a simple message of forgiveness and reconciliation, trying to put into practice on a smaller scale what Mandela and Bishop Tutu were trying to effect in the nation as a whole. She organized small groups, taught trust games, got the prisoners to open up about the details of their horrific childhoods. The year before she began her visits, the prison had recorded 279 acts of violence; the next year there were two. Joanna's results were so impressive that the BBC sent

*It is helpful for everyone to read the Devotional and Scripture Readings and do the My Life with God Exercise before the meeting. Begin the meeting with silent prayer, then move directly to Reflecting on My Life with God below.*

a camera crew from London to produce two one-hour documentaries on her.

I met Joanna and her husband, who has since joined her in the prison work, at a restaurant on the waterfront of Cape Town. Ever the journalist, I pressed her for specifics on what had happened to transform that prison. Her fork stopped on the way to her mouth, she looked up and said, almost without thinking, "Well, of course, Philip, God was already present in the prison. I just had to make him visible."

I have often thought of that line from Joanna, which would make a fine mission statement for all of us seeking to know and follow God. God is already present, in the most unexpected places. We just need to make God visible.[1]


## MY LIFE WITH GOD EXERCISE

Joanna was able to serve God by seeing him in a place where no one else seemed to be looking—a South African prison. Even in that most unexpected place, she found God at work and was quick to join him. Yancey's telling of Joanna's story reveals an essential truth: God is present and working in the circumstances of this world. We have only to train ourselves to see him, not only in the world around us but also in our own hearts, our own lives. In the last chapter, we suggested that if we have never consciously listened for God speaking to us through another person, his voice may be a little hard to hear at first. The same is true for perceiving God's presence in the circumstances in which we find ourselves. Sometimes we recognize his hand almost instantly in an event, or within a short time; other times it may take years, even decades, to realize that God was in a situation and was working in our lives the whole time.

And sometimes we completely miss God's workings in our lives because we just aren't paying attention. We are like the stubborn mule in a well-known story. When the farmer hit the mule over the head with a big board, a neighbor asked him what he was doing. The farmer replied, "Well, first I have to get his attention!" The good news is that we can train ourselves to pay closer attention. In *The God Hunt*, Karen Mains describes how she taught her children to say "I spy God" whenever they realized that God was doing something in their life or someone else's life. Try the same thing this week as you go about your daily routine.

God Stops

Every time you "spy God," write it down or make a mental note of it. You might want to tape reminders (such as "Spy God" or "Keep looking") on the door of your home, on your bathroom mirror, or on the visor of your car, just to make sure you keep up the search. Don't limit yourself to what seems extraordinary or miraculous; also seek God in the details, something that seems like a coincidence or that just brings a smile to your face.

*How did you feel about the "I spy God" exercise? Were you instantly able to spy God working in the circumstances surrounding you or did it take a while? What specific examples of God working had you not recognized before doing the exercise?*

**REFLECTING ON MY LIFE WITH GOD** Allow each member a few moments to answer this question.

▶ **SCRIPTURE READING:** GENESIS 45:4–15; 50:19–20

Then Joseph said to his brothers, "Come closer to me." And they came closer. He said, "I am your brother, Joseph, whom you sold into Egypt. And now do not be distressed, or angry with yourselves, because you sold me here; for God sent me before you to preserve life. For the famine has been in the land these two years; and there are five more years in which there will be neither plowing nor harvest. God sent me before you to preserve for you a remnant on earth, and to keep alive for you many survivors. So it was not you who sent me here, but God; he has made me a father to Pharaoh, and lord of all his house and ruler over all the land of Egypt. Hurry and go up to my father and say to him, 'Thus says your son Joseph, God has made me lord of all Egypt; come down to me, do not delay. You shall settle in the land of Goshen, and you shall be near me, you and your children and your children's children, as well as your flocks, your herds, and all that you have. I will provide for you there—since there are five more years of famine to come—so that you and your household, and all that you have, will not come to poverty.' And now your eyes and the eyes of my brother Benjamin see that it is my own mouth that speaks to you. You must tell my father how greatly I am honored in Egypt, and all that you have seen. Hurry and bring my father down here." Then he fell upon his brother Benjamin's neck and wept, while Benjamin wept upon his neck. And he kissed all his brothers and wept upon them; and after that his brothers talked with him. . . .

After everyone has had a chance to respond to the question, ask a member to read this passage from Scripture.

*Perceiving God in Circumstances*

But Joseph said to [his brothers], "Do not be afraid! Am I in the place of God? Even though you intended to do harm to me, God intended it for good, in order to preserve a numerous people, as he is doing today."

**REFLECTION QUESTION**
Allow each person a few moments to respond to this question.

*Have you ever been hurt or betrayed by another person, particularly someone close to you, and then realized that good actually came out of the painful circumstances?*

more like
game playing

## ▶▶ GETTING THE PICTURE

⬐ After a brief discussion, choose one person to read this section.

In the biblical account of Joseph, we see God working through circumstances to change Joseph's life and the history of an entire nation. The Scriptures you just read tell part of the story of Joseph and his sojourn in Egypt, which saved the family of Israel from extinction and the nation of Egypt from starvation. Let's look at it in more detail.

Joseph is the firstborn of Jacob's favorite wife, Rachel. Jacob, whose name has been changed to Israel, "the one who strives with God," after wrestling with a stranger all night, also plays favorites with his children. In fact, "Israel loved Joseph more than any other of his children, . . . and he had made him a long robe with sleeves" (Gen 37:3). Predictably, this favoritism makes Joseph's brothers extremely jealous.

When Joseph becomes a teenager, he has a dream about eleven bundles of grain bowing down to his bundle of grain. His eleven brothers interpret the dream to mean that Joseph will someday have dominion over them. "So they hated him even more because of his dreams and his words" (v 8b). In Joseph's next dream, "the sun, the moon, and eleven stars were bowing down" to him (v 9b). Joseph tells his brothers about this dream, and their jealousy intensifies. Fearful that he will one day rule over them, the brothers throw Joseph into a pit and then sell him into slavery in Egypt. At first, things go well for Joseph in Egypt; he is made overseer of the house of his master, Potiphar. But when Potiphar's wife unfairly accuses Joseph, he is thrown into prison. However, Joseph's fortune again changes radically when he interprets two of the pharaoh's dreams, and Pharaoh not only releases Joseph from prison but appoints him overseer of all Egypt. When Joseph's brothers come to Egypt begging for food, he greets them from his throne.

## ▶▶▶ GOING DEEPER

✍ Have another member read this section.

We can learn several things about God's ability to work through circumstances from Joseph's story. First, seeing the hand of God is difficult; we do it best in hindsight. Many of us are adept at seeing the hand of God in our blessings: celebrating a special event, recovering from an illness, getting a promotion or a raise. But in other corners of our lives we can be blind to God's subtle workings. When we are fired from a job or turned down by the college of our dreams, we don't see the new and meaningful opportunities that will come our way. Joseph wasn't thinking at the bottom of the pit that his time there was a sign that God was working in his life. It was only when he looked back on his life that he clearly perceived the hand of God in circumstances that had seemed so cruel at the time.

Second, God can work through wonderful *and* awful circumstances. Joseph's treatment in Egypt, as a slave in Potiphar's house and an inmate in Pharaoh's prison, was horrific. The sudden separation from his father and family was terrible for a young man to endure. To say that God is at work in the circumstances in our lives is not to say that everything is ordained by God. The story does not say that God compelled Joseph's brothers to sell him into slavery, only that God was able to work for good within those circumstances. Joseph's brothers had free will, which allowed them not only to make good decisions, acting with unselfishness, courtesy, and humility, but also to fight among themselves and to be ugly to God and to their brother. In today's world we would do well to remember that many of the horrific circumstances we see around us are created by human hands, not divine. Yet God still works even within the most difficult circumstances that we bring about. (See C. S. Lewis's *The Problem of Pain* for a full discussion of God's role in the world.)

Third, even though we often can't perceive God in circumstances while we are going through them, we must maintain our faith that God will bring us out on the other side. By saving his family from starvation, Joseph preserved not only people who would become a great nation, but the ancestors of Jesus. Training ourselves to look for God and his work in our lives helps us know that even if we cannot see his hand in our present circumstances, he is in charge, not us.

*Why is it so much easier to see God's role in our lives when we look back at past events? When you look at the past, in what ways do you see God working? Big events or small ones or both? Do you tend to see God's hand guiding you more through wonderful or horrific circumstances?*

**REFLECTION QUESTION** Allow each person a few moments to respond.

*Perceiving God in Circumstances*

☞ Choose one member
to read this section.

In *Something More,* Catherine Marshall writes about a struggle many of us share: trying to reconcile a great tragedy, such as sickness or death, with our belief that God is somehow with us in everything that happens. When her husband, Peter Marshall, a well-known Christian who had served as the chaplain of the U.S. Senate, died of a coronary occlusion at age forty-six, it threw her faith into turmoil. She could not believe it was God's will for such a thing to happen. When she was finally able to ask God what to do next, she

> was taught one of the greatest lessons any of us can ever learn. . . . Sin is in the world. And sin is "missing the mark," missing God's perfect plan. There is so much of this missing the mark that it is going to impinge on every person's life at some points.
>
> If God left us with only this, real happiness or victory in this life would be an impossible mirage. But the Gospel truly is good news. The news is that there is no situation—no breakage, no loss, no grief, no sin, no mess—so dreadful that out of it God cannot bring good, total good, not just "spiritual" good, if we will allow him to.[2]

After more soul-searching, Marshall felt God tell her that the key was to relinquish all to him and then to praise him for every circumstance, no matter how tragic. It wasn't easy, but the results of her very first attempt serve as a lesson for all of us.

> I began to praise that first time hesitatingly, woodenly: "Lord, I think I'll begin with the small irritations first—that truck driver demolishing the mailbox. Surely, I'm not supposed to thank You for *that!* I can see, Lord, as I talk to You that the mailbox is of no consequence. Looking at You puts petty problems into perspective in a hurry. I can feel Your humor that I took it so seriously. So thank You, Lord, for perspective. Thank You for humor. Thank You for You."
>
> As I persisted down the list, another instruction was given. "Now write down every situation in your life that seems less than good, that you would like to see changed."
>
> That wasn't hard. I went inside to get my red notebook and a pen and proceeded to fill five pages. But what came next *was* hard: "I want you to go down the list and praise Me for every item."

"Lord, I can see praising You for bringing good out of all these things, but I still don't understand how I can praise You for the bad things. Doesn't that make You the Author of Evil?"

"I am Lord over all—good and evil. You start praising. I'll supply the understanding."

Step by hesitant step, I was being led on an exciting spiritual adventure.[3]

## ▶▶▶▶▶ GOING FORWARD

In the biblical story of Joseph and in Catherine Marshall's experiences with God, we see the truth of Paul's statement: "We know that all things work together for good for those who love God, who are called according to his purpose" (Rom 8:28). God truly is working at all times in our lives, if, as Joanna pointed out in the Devotional Reading, only we have eyes to see him. We challenge ourselves to train our senses to see God. We try Catherine Marshall's experiment of praising God for everything in our life that seems less than praiseworthy. We continue playing "I spy God." Every glimpse we get into God's activity around us better equips us to join him in his kingdom work, just as Joanna did in the South African prison.

*Have another person read this section.*

But there are still times when we cannot perceive God's hand. Often these are times of challenge and difficulty, when we can see God's role only with hindsight. When our circumstances are unfavorable, when the world seems to be set against us, we have to remember that this does not mean that God is not with us working for good. God can work through all kinds of circumstances, good and bad. The most important thing is to have faith that God's hand is with us, even if we cannot feel it. An inscription found on a cellar wall in Germany where Jews hid from Nazis describes faith of this kind: "I believe in the sun even when it is not shining. I believe in love even when feeling it not. I believe in God even when he is silent."[4]

*In what difficult events in your life or in the world around you are you still having trouble discerning God's role?*

**REFLECTION QUESTION**
Again, allow each member a few moments to answer this question.

This concludes our look at perceiving God in circumstances. In the next chapter we will turn our attention to another avenue of connecting with God—seeking God in silence.

*After everyone has had a chance to respond, the leader reads this paragraph.*

Allow some time for members to encourage one another to read the Devotional and Scripture Readings and do the exercise in the following chapter before the next meeting. Then invite the members to be silent for a few moments before leading them in reading the Closing Prayer aloud together.

At the end of the Closing Prayer, the leader asks for a volunteer to lead the next meeting.

## CLOSING PRAYER

To you, O LORD, I lift up my soul.
Make me to know your ways, O LORD;
    teach me your paths.
Lead me in your truth, and teach me,
    for you are the God of my salvation,
    for you I wait all day long.
"Come," my heart says, "seek his face!"
    Your face, LORD, do I seek.
Give ear to my words, O LORD;
    give heed to my sighing.
Listen to the sound of my cry,
    my King and my God,
    for to you I pray. Amen. (PSS 25:1, 4–5; 27:8; 5:1–2)


## TAKING IT FURTHER

**ADDITIONAL EXERCISES**

- Interview two people who have been particularly sensitive to God's work in their lives. Your interview subjects can be anyone—a parent, neighbor, pastor, or friend. Some questions you might ask them: How did you choose your vocation? What training did you get that prepared you for your job? How do you go about seeing the hand of God in your circumstances? Was there ever a time when you thought God was not involved in what you did? Then ask yourself the same questions and write down the answers, taking care to be honest with yourself. After hearing another person's testimony about how God has been working or not working in their life, you will probably be surprised at what you discover about yourself.

- Take time over several nights to record the ways God has been present in the circumstances of your life, past and present. You might focus each night on a certain period of your life, for example, childhood, high school, college, parenthood, your first job, retirement. Pull out some old photo albums or old journals to help you remember the people and places that touched your life at that time. Try to contrast the way you felt about events at the time and the way you look at them now, with the advantage of hindsight.

Lewis, C. S. *The Problem of Pain.* San Francisco: HarperSanFrancisco, 1940.

Marshall, Catherine. *Something More: In Search of a Deeper Faith.* New York: Avon, 1974.

Yancey, Philip. *Finding God in Unexpected Places.* Rev. ed. New York: Doubleday, 2005.

*How do you think Joseph's brothers felt when he revealed his identity to them? Do you think it changed their feelings to hear that God intended their actions for good?*

*Who do you relate to in Joseph's story, Joseph or his brothers? Why?*

*Have you ever been able to see God's hand at work in circumstances while they were happening, without the benefit of hindsight? If so, were they happy or difficult circumstances? Why might that make a difference?*

# SEEKING GOD IN SILENCE

7

## DEVOTIONAL READING

THOMAS À KEMPIS, *The Imitation of Christ*

### *Of the Love of Solitude and Silence*

Seek a proper time to be at leisure with yourself, and think often of God's kindness. Leave curiosity alone. Read subjects that touch the heart rather than those that pass the time. If you will avoid needless talk and idle visits and not listen for the latest gossip, you will find plenty of suitable time for good meditations. The greatest saints guarded their time alone and chose to serve God in solitude. Someone has said, "As often as I went out among men, I returned less of a man." We often experience this when we have spent a long time in idle chatter. It is easier to be completely silent than not to be long-winded; it is easier to stay at home than to be properly on guard outside the monastery. A person whose goal is the inward, spiritual life must cast his lot with Jesus and not follow the crowd.

No one is secure except the person who freely keeps to himself. No one speaks securely except the person who willingly keeps silent. No one leads securely except the person who freely serves. No one commands securely except the person who thoroughly obeys. No one knows secure joy except the person who holds a good conscience in his own heart....

In silence and peace a devout soul makes progress and learns the secrets of the scriptures. Only in silence and peace does a devout soul find floods of tears in which it may wash and cleanse itself each night. The further the soul is from the noise of the world, the closer it may be

✍ It is helpful for everyone to read the Devotional and Scripture Readings and do the My Life with God Exercise before the meeting. Begin the meeting with silent prayer, then move directly to Reflecting on My Life with God below.

to its Creator, for God, with his holy angels, will draw close to a person who seeks solitude and silence.[1]

## MY LIFE WITH GOD EXERCISE

Here Thomas à Kempis suggests that we voluntarily take time off from our work and daily routine to spend some time with God. Part of this involves meditating in silence. Although Thomas wrote in the fifteenth century, his call to silence seems more apt today than ever, in a world where it seems like we are never free from noise, whether it's the obvious sounds of TVs, radios, or iPods or more subtle background sounds, such as traffic or the humming of refrigerators and computers. But he calls us to another type of silence as well. He recommends that we avoid idle conversation and gossip, and that we hold our tongues, because it's "easier to be completely silent than not to be long-winded."

This week, try to set aside ten minutes every day just to sit before God. Choose a place where there is as little noise as possible—and quietly sit. Don't read. Try not to look out a window. Imagine that you are in Elijah's cave. (See 1 Kings 19:1–16.) If you've never done this before, it will be hard to keep your mind from talking about what you should be doing, the time you're wasting, and the deadlines you have to meet. It is a time to make the nagger within—that voice that's always harping, "Do this, do that"—obey you. Quietly, silently, give this chatter to the Lord. After the chatter has died down, focus on listening. If you hear something, don't write it down, because this is time to "waste" for the Lord. If you fall asleep, don't feel bad! Maybe God wanted to give you some needed rest. Try again the next day.

If it feels right as you go about your week, carry that silence over into your daily routine. Be cautious about speaking. Say only what is needed in every conversation. If you have a job that requires a lot of talking, take a minute or so every hour to cease all conversation. Shut the door to your office if you have to, or go for a short walk. As you're doing both sides of the exercise, continually monitor how you feel about "wasting" time for God and refraining from talking.

**REFLECTING ON MY LIFE WITH GOD**
Allow each member a few moments to answer this question.

*On a scale of one to ten, with one being very easy and ten very hard, how difficult was this exercise? Which was the hardest—setting aside ten minutes a day to be silent before the Lord or confining conversation to the barest essentials? What feelings about the silence or lack of silence were most prominent*

*Concealment – mus wandering*

*as you did these two small exercises? What spiritual needs or problems did you discover?*

➤ **SCRIPTURE READING:** 1 KINGS 19:1–16

Ahab told Jezebel all that Elijah had done, and how he had killed all the prophets with the sword. Then Jezebel sent a messenger to Elijah, saying, "So may the gods do to me, and more also, if I do not make your life like the life of one of them by this time tomorrow." Then [Elijah] was afraid; he got up and fled for his life, and came to Beer-sheba, which belongs to Judah; he left his servant there.

But he himself went a day's journey into the wilderness, and came and sat down under a solitary broom tree. He asked that he might die: "It is enough; now, O LORD, take away my life, for I am no better than my ancestors." Then he lay down under the broom tree and fell asleep. Suddenly an angel touched him and said to him, "Get up and eat." He looked, and there at his head was a cake baked on hot stones, and a jar of water. He ate and drank, and lay down again. The angel of the LORD came a second time, touched him, and said, "Get up and eat, otherwise the journey will be too much for you." He got up, and ate and drank; then he went in the strength of that food forty days and forty nights to Horeb the mount of God. At that place he came to a cave, and spent the night there.

Then the word of the LORD came to him, saying, "What are you doing here, Elijah?" He answered, "I have been very zealous for the LORD, the God of hosts; for the Israelites have forsaken your covenant, thrown down your altars, and killed your prophets with the sword. I alone am left, and they are seeking my life, to take it away."

He said, "Go out and stand on the mountain before the LORD, for the LORD is about to pass by." Now there was a great wind, so strong that it was splitting mountains and breaking rocks in pieces before the LORD, but the LORD was not in the wind; and after the wind an earthquake, but the LORD was not in the earthquake; and after the earthquake a fire, but the LORD was not in the fire; and after the fire a sound of sheer silence. When Elijah heard it, he wrapped his face in his mantle and went out and stood at the entrance of the cave. Then there came a voice to him that said, "What are you doing here, Elijah?" He answered, "I have been very zealous for the LORD, the God of hosts; for the Israelites

✍ After everyone has had a chance to respond to the question, ask a member to read this passage from Scripture.

have forsaken your covenant, thrown down your altars, and killed your prophets with the sword. I alone am left, and they are seeking my life, to take it away." Then the LORD said to him, "Go ... you shall anoint Jehu son of Nimshi as king over Israel; and you shall anoint Elisha son of Shaphat of Abel-meholah as prophet in your place."

**REFLECTION QUESTION**
Allow each person a few moments to respond to this question.

*How have you experienced God's presence when you were in despair, like Elijah?* Underneath the everlasting arms

## ►► GETTING THE PICTURE

🗩 After a brief discussion, choose one person to read this section.

When we first meet Elijah, a prophet of the Lord, he predicts to Ahab, the king of the northern kingdom of Israel, that "there shall be neither dew nor rain these years, except by my word" (1 Kings 17:1). This action seems to add fuel to the long-standing enmity between Elijah and Jezebel, Ahab's wife and a worshipper of Baal, who ordered the murder of the prophets of the Lord. After this prediction, God sends Elijah into the wilderness for the first time, to a place so remote that the ravens have to feed him. But while Ahab's kingdom suffers the terrible drought, God provides for Elijah, first through the ravens and a nearby stream and then through a widow living in a town close by.

After a time, God tells Elijah that the drought will cease and instructs him to present himself to Ahab. At this meeting, Elijah tells Ahab that he has "forsaken the commandments of the LORD and followed the Baals" (18:18). Elijah then challenges Ahab to gather all Israel and the prophets of Baal and Asherah at Mount Carmel. On Mount Carmel, Elijah gives the people a choice: follow Baal or the Lord. No one says a word. Elijah then asks the people to bring him two bulls, one for himself and one for the prophets of Baal. Elijah and the prophets lay their bulls on the wood. The prophets call on Baal to provide the fire for their sacrifice; Elijah calls on the Lord.

But when the prophets call on Baal, nothing happens: "There was no voice, no answer, and no response" (v 29). In contrast, when Elijah prepares the altar and prays to the Lord, "the fire of the LORD fell and consumed the burnt offering, the wood, the stones, and the dust, and even licked up the water that was in the trench" (v 38). The people of Israel fall on their faces and acknowledge that "the LORD indeed is God." Elijah has the people take the prophets of Baal to the Wadi Kishon, where he kills them. Then he tells Ahab to go home and eat and drink because the drought will be ending, a message that is confirmed when Elijah's servant sees "a little cloud no bigger than a person's hand" rising out of the sea (v 44). When Ahab arrives at the palace, he tells Jezebel "all that Elijah had done," which sets in motion Jezebel's angry message to Elijah and his second flight into the wilderness.

Perhaps the wilderness appeals to Elijah because of his earlier experience, when God provided for him in a similarly lonely place. In any case, he needs to escape Jezebel's threat, so he travels south over ninety miles to the wilderness beyond Beer-sheba, where he recovers from the showdown with the prophets of Baal and his long trip and has another intimate encounter with God.

## ▶▶▶ GOING DEEPER

The first thing we notice in the story of Elijah is that his public life as a prophet was balanced with times of "hiddenness." His life thus had a certain balance. Between encounters with Ahab and the prophets of Baal, we see Elijah spending times of solitude in a far place. This is a pattern we see throughout the Bible. From God speaking to Moses on Mount Sinai to Jesus's forty days in the wilderness, God uses private time in a desolate place to prepare those he chooses for leadership roles. There are other clear parallels between the three stories. Not only is the time period of forty days and forty nights repeated—the time Jesus spent in the wilderness, the time it took Moses to write down God's covenant, the time it took Elijah to travel to the cave—but Elijah's cave was on the same mountain where God gave the law to Moses. In each case, time in the quiet of the wilderness strengthened the person for the challenges ahead.

We also see that Elijah's time in the wilderness prepared him for his encounter with the Lord. In the solitude of the wilderness, he had no choice but to depend upon the Lord for his sustenance, both food and rest. Although Elijah, like us, was dependent on God at all times, it was easier to pay attention to that fact when other distractions were removed. Elijah could not fail to notice God's provisions in the wilderness near Beer-sheba, one of the few places in Judah with nourishing plant life and wild animals. In addition to food and rest, Elijah found silence for the nurture of his soul. It was far from the din of Baal's prophets pleading with their god to set fire to their sacrifice. This is also Thomas

✍ Have another member read this section.

à Kempis's insight into the spiritual life: "Whoever wants to arrive at interiority and spirituality has to leave the crowd."

Elijah's story teaches us that time spent alone in silence and solitude can be difficult but also restorative. Even after God triumphed over the prophets of Baal, when Jezebel threatened Elijah's life, Elijah became discouraged and filled with despair. Much like us when hard times hit, he gave up: "It is enough; now, O LORD, take away my life, for I am no better than my ancestors" (19:4b). The encounter with the prophets of Baal and the journey to the wilderness of Beer-sheba had exhausted him not only physically but also mentally and emotionally. It took two meals for Elijah to gain the physical strength to make the forty-day journey to Mount Horeb (Sinai). From all indications, he was still not quite ready for God to appear to him after his arrival, because he needed to rest that night in a cave. But despite his discouragement and depression, the solitude and silence of the journey and the night in the cave prepared Elijah to listen for God.

In the end, God's voice was heard in the silence. God is in the silence. Silence can be heard. This may be a foreign concept for us today in the midst of a culture that values noise over silence, but those of us who grew up on farms and ranches and in rural areas know it is true. Silence is palpable. The words translated "sheer silence" in verse 12b can also be translated "a gentle whisper" (NIV) or "a still small voice" (KJV). Elijah's silence was filled with God's presence. And in this silence Elijah heard God's voice.

**REFLECTION QUESTION**
Allow each person a few
moments to respond.

*What are some times in your own life when you heard God's voice speaking to you in an atmosphere of silence?*

Shower

## ▶▶▶▶ POINTING TO GOD

Choose one member
to read this section.

Perhaps more than any other contemporary Christian, Thomas Merton understood the value of silence. A Trappist monk in rural Kentucky, Merton spent much of his life looking for God in the quietness of the monastic life and writing about his insights in such books as *Thoughts in Solitude* and *Dialogues with Silence*. Just as Thomas à Kempis wrote about the limits of talking, so Merton found that even in prayer, silence was often best. One of his simplest prayers beautifully expresses this idea:

CONNECTING WITH GOD

My God, I pray better to You by breathing.
I pray better to You by walking than by talking.[2]

Ultimately, Merton, like Elijah, seems to come to the conclusion that silence is not just a condition we cultivate in order to better hear the word of God, but that *silence itself is where we find God*. In one of his last books, *The Climate of Monastic Prayer,* he writes,

> The true contemplative is not one who prepares his mind for a particular message that he wants or expects to hear, but is one who remains empty because he knows that he can never expect to anticipate the words that will transform his darkness into light. He does not even anticipate a special kind of transformation. He does not demand light instead of darkness. He waits on the Word of God in silence, and, when he is "answered," it is not so much by a word that bursts into his silence. It is by his silence itself, suddenly, inexplicably revealing itself to him as a word of great power, full of the voice of God.[3]

## ▶▶▶▶ GOING FORWARD

The words of Thomas à Kempis and Thomas Merton and the experience of Elijah all speak of the power of finding God through time spent in solitude and silence. God uses silence to prepare us for ministry, to speak to us. Yet most of us set aside embarrassingly little time to stop talking about it and actually be quiet with God. Our situations may be very different from that of Elijah, whose last resort was to go into the silence of the wilderness to save his own life. But being so trapped in the everyday responsibilities of life that we don't feel like we can "waste" time being silent before God can be just as desperate a situation. Without periods of silence, our souls shrivel up and die. We may not be facing physical death like Elijah did, but we come face-to-face with spiritual atrophy when our lives are filled with constant noise from which there is no respite.

Maybe we find so many excuses because to be alone with nothing but the sound of our own souls is, frankly, a frightening prospect. In the quiet we can no longer avoid complicated questions about the direction of our lives or more frightening topics, like our own mortality. When we're no longer talking, God can direct our thoughts in the way

✍ Have another person read this section.

*Seeking God in Silence*

69

he wishes, not the way we wish. It is yet another way of giving up the reins of our life to God—not something many of us are very good at. Deep down, however, we all know that he is the only one we can trust with them. "For God alone my soul waits in silence, for my hope is from him" (Ps 62:5).

**REFLECTION QUESTION**
Again, allow each member a few moments to answer this question.

*Do you relish silence or does it make you uncomfortable? If silence is uncomfortable for you, why do you think that is? What might you do to overcome that?*

🕊 After everyone has had a chance to respond, the leader reads this paragraph.

This concludes our look at seeking God in silence. In the next chapter we will turn our attention to another avenue of connecting with God—seeing him in dreams and visions.

🕊 **Allow some time for members to encourage one another to read the Devotional and Scripture Readings and do the exercise in the following chapter before the next meeting.** Then invite the members to be silent for a few moments before leading them in reading the Closing Prayer aloud together.

## CLOSING PRAYER

To you, O LORD, I lift up my soul.
Make me to know your ways, O LORD;
    teach me your paths.
Lead me in your truth, and teach me,
    for you are the God of my salvation,
    for you I wait all day long.
"Come," my heart says, "seek his face!"
    Your face, LORD, do I seek.
Give ear to my words, O LORD;
    give heed to my sighing.
Listen to the sound of my cry,
    my King and my God,
    for to you I pray. Amen. (PSS 25:1, 4–5; 27:8; 5:1–2)

🕊 At the end of the Closing Prayer, the leader asks for a volunteer to lead the next meeting.

## TAKING IT FURTHER

**ADDITIONAL EXERCISE**

Go on a silent retreat of two days or more. (It can take a day or so just to get accustomed to the silence.) You might look for monasteries in your area where you can stay, or check into a structured silent retreat at a conference center. If you would like to plan your own silent retreat, Emilie Griffin's *Wilderness Time* is a good resource.

Griffin, Emilie. *Wilderness Time: A Guide for Spiritual Retreat.* San
    Francisco: HarperSanFrancisco, 1997.
Merton, Thomas. *Dialogues with Silence: Prayers & Drawings.* Edited by
    Jonathan Montaldo. San Francisco: HarperSanFrancisco, 2001.
Thomas à Kempis. *The Imitation of Christ.* Translated by William C.
    Creasy. Notre Dame, IN: Ave Maria Press, 1989.

**ADDITIONAL RESOURCES**

*In your own life, is there a balance between periods of being in public and
periods of being hidden? How might you address the imbalance, if there is one?*

**ADDITIONAL REFLECTION
QUESTIONS**

*What in your life might serve as a retreat to the wilderness? What such
retreats have you experienced in the past?*

*How does your prayer differ when you are in public from when you are alone, in silence?*

# SEEING GOD IN DREAMS AND VISIONS

**8**

KEY SCRIPTURE: Genesis 28:10–22

## DEVOTIONAL READING

TERESA OF AVILA, *The Life of St. Teresa of Jesus, of the Order of Our Lady of Carmel*

I now resume the story of my life. I was in great pain and distress; and many prayers, as I said, were made on my behalf, that our Lord would lead me by another and a safer way.... At the end of two years spent in prayer by myself and others ... this happened to me. I was in prayer one day ... when I saw Christ close by me, or, to speak more correctly, felt Him; for I saw nothing with the eyes of the body, nothing with the eyes of the soul. He seemed to me to be close beside me; and I saw, too, as I believe, that it was He who was speaking to me.... Jesus Christ seemed to be by my side continually, and, as the vision was not imaginary, I saw no form; but I had a most distinct feeling that He was always on my right hand, a witness of all I did; and never at any time, if I was but slightly recollected, or not too much distracted, could I be ignorant of His near presence....

    I spent some days, not many, with that vision continually before me. It did me so much good, that I never ceased to pray. Even when I did cease, I contrived that it should be in such a way as that I should not displease Him whom I saw so clearly present, an eye-witness of my acts. And though I was occasionally afraid, because so much was said to me about delusions, that fear lasted not long, because our Lord assured me.

    It pleased our Lord, one day that I was in prayer, to show me His Hands, and His Hands only. The beauty of them was so great, that no language can describe it. This put me in great fear; for everything that is strange, in the beginning of any new grace from God makes me very much afraid. A few days later, I saw His divine Face, and I was utterly

> It is helpful for everyone to read the Devotional and Scripture Readings and do the My Life with God Exercise before the meeting. Begin the meeting with silent prayer, then move directly to Reflecting on My Life with God below.

entranced. I could not understand why our Lord showed Himself in this way, seeing that, afterwards, He granted me the grace of seeing His whole Person. . . .

On one of the feasts . . . there stood before me the most Sacred Humanity . . . in great beauty and majesty. . . . This vision, though imaginary, I never saw with my bodily eyes, nor indeed, any other, but only with the eyes of the soul. Those who understand these things better than I do, say that the intellectual vision is more perfect than this; and this, the imaginary vision, much more perfect than those visions which are seen by the bodily eyes. . . . It is true that afterwards the vision is forgotten; but there remains so deep an impression of the majesty and beauty of God, that it is impossible to forget it. . . . The soul is itself no longer, it is always inebriated; it seems as if a living love of God, of the highest kind, made a new beginning with it. . . . These two kinds of visions come almost always together; and they do so come; for we behold the excellency and beauty and glory of the most Holy Humanity with the eyes of the soul. And in the other way I have spoken of,—that of intellectual vision,—we learn how He is God, is mighty, can do all things, commands all things, governs all things, and fills all things with His love.[1]

## MY LIFE WITH GOD EXERCISE

On Pentecost after the resurrection of Jesus and the pouring out of the Holy Spirit upon the disciples, the apostle Peter quoted the prophet Joel in his sermon to the crowd that gathered:

> In the last days it will be, God declares,
>   that I will pour out my Spirit upon all flesh,
>       and your sons and your daughters shall prophesy
>   and your young men shall see visions,
>       and your old men shall dream dreams. (ACTS 2:17, JOEL 2:28)

In spite of this clear promise, some today do not believe that Christians receive dreams and visions from God. Since the skepticism about dreams and visions in Western Christianity runs so deep and it is impossible to design an exercise that will enable all of us to experience dreams or visions from God, we ask you to read some Scriptures that describe such experiences. We are not going to recommend a reading schedule, just that you read at least three of the selections below before the next meeting. As you read the passages, think about what characteristics, if any, differentiate a vision from a dream. Also pay attention to the relationship between God and the person who receives the dream or vision, and how the person responds to the communication.

## Dreams and Visions

| | |
|---|---|
| Genesis 15:1–21 | Daniel 2:1–48 |
| Genesis 20:1–18 | Daniel 4:4–27 |
| Genesis 31:10–24 | Daniel 7 |
| Genesis 37:5–11 | Daniel 8 |
| Genesis 40:5–19 | Daniel 10:2ff |
| Genesis 41:1–36 | Zechariah 1:1–6:8 |
| Genesis 46:1–7 | Matthew 1:20–24 |
| Joshua 5:13–15 | Matthew 2:12–23 |
| Judges 7:13–18 | Matthew 17:1–13 |
| 1 Kings 3:5–15 | Matthew 27:19 |
| Psalm 89:19–37 | Acts 9:10–19 |
| Isaiah 6 | Acts 10:9–33 |
| Jeremiah 38:19–23 | Acts 16:9–10 |
| Ezekiel 1 ff. | Acts 18:9–11 |
| Ezekiel 8–11 | Revelation |
| Ezekiel 40–48 | |

*What were some things you noticed about these Scriptures? What was the purpose of the messages? What did the visions and dreams have in common? How did God use them? Were there times when they effected change? If so, what was the change?*

REFLECTING ON MY LIFE WITH GOD
Allow each member a few moments to answer this question.

▶ **SCRIPTURE READING:** GENESIS 28:10–22

Jacob left Beer-sheba and went toward Haran. He came to a certain place and stayed there for the night, because the sun had set. Taking one of the stones of the place, he put it under his head and lay down in that place. And he dreamed that there was a ladder set up on the earth, the top of it reaching to heaven; and the angels of God were ascending and descending on it. And the LORD stood beside him and said, "I am the LORD, the

After everyone has had a chance to respond to the question, ask a member to read this passage from Scripture.

God of Abraham your father and the God of Isaac; the land on which you lie I will give to you and to your offspring; and your offspring shall be like the dust of the earth, and you shall spread abroad to the west and to the east and to the north and to the south; and all the families of the earth shall be blessed in you and in your offspring. Know that I am with you and will keep you wherever you go, and will bring you back to this land; for I will not leave you until I have done what I have promised you." Then Jacob woke from his sleep and said, "Surely the LORD is in this place—and I did not know it!" And he was afraid, and said, "How awesome is this place! This is none other than the house of God, and this is the gate of heaven."

So Jacob rose early in the morning, and he took the stone that he had put under his head and set it up for a pillar and poured oil on the top of it. He called that place Bethel; but the name of the city was Luz at the first. Then Jacob made a vow, saying, "If God will be with me, and will keep me in this way that I go, and will give me bread to eat and clothing to wear, so that I come again to my father's house in peace, then the LORD shall be my God, and this stone, which I have set up for a pillar, shall be God's house; and of all that you give me I will surely give one-tenth to you."

*seldom*

**REFLECTION QUESTION**
Allow each person a few moments to respond to this question.

*How often do you remember your dreams? Have you ever had a dream in which God spoke to you as he did to Jacob, or a vision like Teresa's?*

*Rachel*

## ▶▶ GETTING THE PICTURE

After a brief discussion, choose one person to read this section.

Jacob is the second of twins born to Isaac and Rebekah. When Rebekah was pregnant, Jacob and his older brother, Esau, "struggled together within her," a portent of their lifelong strife (Gen 25:22). Though younger than Esau, Jacob, whose name means "He supplants" or "He takes by the heel," secures the birthright—all of the privileges of the eldest son—when Esau trades it for a bowl of stew. Later, Jacob tricks his father into thinking he is Esau and receives Isaac's blessing:

> May God give you of the dew of heaven,
> and of the fatness of the earth,
> and plenty of grain and wine.

CONNECTING WITH GOD

> Let peoples serve you,
>> and nations bow down to you.
> Be lord over your brothers,
>> and may your mother's sons bow down
>> to you. (27:28–29)

When Esau comes to receive his blessing, Isaac tells him that he has already given it to Jacob, and thus Jacob will be his master. Esau begs and weeps for a blessing, and his father Isaac answers him:

> See, away from the fatness of the earth
>> shall your home be,
> and away from the dew of heaven on high.
> By your sword you shall live,
>> and you shall serve your brother;
> but when you break loose,
>> you shall break his yoke from your neck. (27:39–40)

Upon seeing how angry Esau is at Jacob for deceiving their father and receiving the blessing, Rebekah and Jacob arrange for him to flee to her brother, Laban. As Jacob is traveling from Beer-sheba to Haran, a distance of about five hundred miles, he has the dream.

## ▶▶▶ GOING DEEPER

There are many similarities between Jacob's dream and Teresa of Avila's vision. They were both in distress, Jacob because Esau's plan to kill him was forcing him to leave the land of his birth, Teresa because she had prayed desperately for change in her life but it hadn't happened. Neither Jacob nor Teresa had any hint that God would appear to them. From all appearances, Jacob's trip was going as planned. Esau hadn't pursued him, and Jacob had already traveled about fifty miles. He might have felt safe when he reached Bethel and heaved a sigh of relief. Though Teresa had been praying for years, she didn't expect that change would be preceded by the presence and vision of Christ. Both Jacob's dream and Teresa's vision were initiated by God. Jacob and Teresa had nothing to do with the content or timing or length. Finally, they both recognized that their experience was sacred. Jacob anointed the rock that he had used for a pillow and then made a vow to God. Teresa's vision drew her closer to the Lord, so that she prayed continuously and never forgot the experience.

*Have another member read this section.*

Jacob's dream and Teresa's vision show us that, when it comes to dreams and visions, we cannot predict, initiate, or even prompt them. Amazingly, they come to those with exemplary prayer lives, such as Teresa, and to those who strike us more as exemplary sinners, such as Jacob. Perhaps emotional states like distress or desperation, or preparation, such as long periods of prayer or fasting (Dan 10:2–3), make us more receptive to such communications, but there is no guarantee that any action on our part can provoke a dream or vision from God. Dreams and visions are yet another area in which we must assent to God's control. Unlike many other ways of communicating with God, we cannot initiate or even practice communicating with God in this way. All we can do is stay open to the possibility.

As you may have noticed in the passages from Scripture in this exercise, and in Jacob's and Teresa's responses to their experiences, many who have gone before us have cultivated an openness to hearing God through dreams and visions. Both Teresa and Jacob immediately recognized that their experiences were of God, and acted accordingly. These experiences changed the direction of their lives. Even those recorded in Scripture who did not worship God (kings, the Egyptian pharaoh, the prisoners in jail with Joseph) were open to at least the prophetic aspect of dreams. Perhaps it was because their religious practices made them open to hearing God (or gods) in this way. Or maybe it is because they lived in a pre-Enlightenment world. Today, one of our challenges is keeping ourselves open to this form of God's communication.

**REFLECTION QUESTION**
Allow each person a few moments to respond.

*If you have ever experienced a dream or a vision that you believe was from God, how did you know it was from God? How did you respond to it? If you have not had this experience, how do you think you might respond to such a communication?*

### ▶▶▶▶ POINTING TO GOD

✍ Choose one member to read this section.

It cannot be emphasized enough that there is no reason not to assume that all of the ways God communicates to us in the Bible are still available channels for modern-day Christians. God has not stopped communicating with his people through dreams and visions. One striking modern-day example is the experience of writer Brennan Manning. One day Manning was praying in his room at a retreat center and feeling overcome with self-hatred, a litany of his sins playing in his head:

> Praying over the passage of the washing of the feet (John 13:1–17), I was suddenly transported in faith into the Upper Room, where I took Judas's place among the Twelve. The Servant, who had tied a towel round his waist, poured water from a pitcher into a copper basin and reached out to wash my feet (the dress and duty those of a slave). Involuntarily I pulled my foot back. I couldn't look at him. I had betrayed the vision, been unfaithful to my dream (and thus unfaithful to his plan for my life).
>
> Sensing my dismay, he placed his hand on my knee and said, "Brennan, do you know what these years together have meant to me? You were being held even when you didn't believe I was holding you. I love you, my friend."
>
> Tears rolled down my cheeks. "But Lord, my sins, my repeated failures, my weaknesses . . ."
>
> "I understand. Brennan, I expected more failure from you than you expected from yourself." He smiled. "And you always came back. Nothing pleases me as much as when you trust me, when you allow that my compassion is bigger than your sinfulness."
>
> "But Jesus, what about my irritating character defects—the boasting, the inflating of the truth, the pretense of being an intellectual, the impatience with people, and all the times I drank to excess?"
>
> "What you are saying is true. But your love for me has never wavered: your heart has remained pure. What's more, even in the darkness and confusion, you've always done something that overshadowed all the rest. You were kind to sinners."
>
> I cried—so loudly that the retreatant in the adjacent room knocked on the door to ask if I was all right.
>
> "Now I'll go," Jesus said. "I've just washed your feet. Do the same for others. Serve my people humbly and lovingly. You will find happiness if you do. Peace, my friend."[2]

## ⮞⮞⮞⮞ GOING FORWARD

Here we have three very different examples of God communicating with human beings through visions and dreams. From the mystical vision

🖎 Have another person read this section.

of Teresa to the life-changing dream Jacob received while on the run to Manning's vision of the Upper Room and his conversation with Jesus, God spoke to these three people in radically diverse ways. Teresa mentions no words in her description of her vision, only that she felt God's presence and eventually saw Jesus, first his hands, then his face, and finally his "entire person." Jacob had a vision and received a message from God. Manning had a vision *and* a conversation with Jesus. Each also reacted differently. Teresa felt some fear but also relates that the vision did her much good. Jacob responded with action, consecrating a stone and making a vow to God. Manning's initial response was to weep.

It's tempting to dismiss dreams and visions as one-way experiences: God chooses to give us a vision or dream and then we passively receive it. Indeed, we have discussed the fact that we cannot initiate or prompt a dream or vision from God. However, that doesn't mean there is nothing we can do. All ways of communicating with God are interrelated. As we grow closer to God in prayer, by study of the Scriptures, appreciation of his creation, and participating in corporate worship, we open ourselves to other ways of experiencing him. Commitment and intention of the heart are important. Some words of Thomas Merton regarding contemplation are appropriate here:

> The fact remains that contemplation will not be given to those who willfully remain at a distance from God, who confine their interior life to a few routine exercises of piety and a few external acts of worship and service performed as a matter of duty. Such people are careful to avoid sin. They respect God as a Master. But their hearts do not belong to Him. They are not really interested in Him, except in order to insure themselves against losing heaven and going to hell. In actual practice, their minds and hearts are taken up with their own ambitions and troubles and comforts and pleasures and all their worldly interest and anxieties and fears. God is only invited to enter this charmed circle to smooth out difficulties and to dispense rewards.[3]

Who among us doesn't feel the sting of these words? A relationship of intimate communion with God is possible, but it requires investment and sacrifice on our part. Some of us may never experience the kind of dreams or visions detailed in this chapter. In fact, it is certain that God will not communicate with us exactly the way he communicated with Teresa or Jacob or Brennan Manning. But the good news is that if we open our hearts and minds to him, we can expect God to communicate with us in some way.

*If you had a vision and conversation with Jesus like the one Brennan Manning experienced, what would you talk about? How do you think you would respond to having a conversation with Jesus in person?*

**REFLECTION QUESTION**
Again, allow each member a few moments to answer this question.

This concludes our look at dreams and visions. In the next chapter we will turn our attention to another avenue of communicating with God—sensing his presence.

✐ After everyone has had a chance to respond, the leader reads this paragraph.

## CLOSING PRAYER

To you, O LORD, I lift up my soul.
Make me to know your ways, O LORD;
    teach me your paths.
Lead me in your truth, and teach me,
    for you are the God of my salvation,
    for you I wait all day long.
"Come," my heart says, "seek his face!"
    Your face, LORD, do I seek.
Give ear to my words, O LORD;
    give heed to my sighing.
Listen to the sound of my cry,
    my King and my God,
    for to you I pray. Amen. (PSS 25:1, 4–5; 27:8; 5:1–2)

✐ Allow some time for members to encourage one another to read the Devotional and Scripture Readings and do the exercise in the following chapter before the next meeting. Then invite the members to be silent for a few moments before leading them in reading the Closing Prayer aloud together.

✐ At the end of the Closing Prayer, the leader asks for a volunteer to lead the next meeting.

## TAKING IT FURTHER

Keep a notebook and pen beside your bed to record any dreams you may remember when you wake up. Obviously, not all dreams have significance. Some will be easily understood as a reflection of your own emotions or fears (i.e., dreaming about an unexpected test at school or an upcoming event that you are nervous about). But record what you can remember, and as you write down each dream, ask God to help you to identify and interpret any messages he may have for you.

**ADDITIONAL EXERCISE**

Manning, Brennan. *A Glimpse of Jesus: The Stranger to Self-Hatred.* San
    Francisco: HarperSanFrancisco, 2003.
Spangler, Ann. *Dreams: True Stories of Remarkable Encounters with God.*
    Grand Rapids, MI: Zondervan, 1997.

**ADDITIONAL RESOURCES**

Teresa of Avila, *The Life of St. Teresa of Jesus, of the Order of Our Lady of Carmel.* Translated by David Lewis. New York: Benziger Bros., 1904.
Teresa of Avila, *Interior Castle.* Translated by E. Allison Peers. New York: Doubleday/Image, 1972.

**ADDITIONAL REFLECTION QUESTIONS**

*How common do you think it is to see God in dreams and visions? Do you think God may have spoken to you in a dream, but you forgot the dream or failed to understand the message? Do you think people have vision or dream experiences of God but perhaps don't discuss them? Explain.*

*How would you compare dreams and visions with other ways God communicates with us?*

*If you've ever had a dream or vision you believe was from God, what were the circumstances leading up to your experience? Was it a particularly difficult time or a time in which you had been actively seeking a word from God? What did you learn about opening yourself to God?*

# SENSING GOD'S PRESENCE

9

**KEY SCRIPTURE: Joshua 2:1–15; 6:16b, 17, 23a, 25a**

## DEVOTIONAL READING

C. S. LEWIS, *A Grief Observed*

No one ever told me that grief felt so like fear. I am not afraid, but the sensation is like being afraid. The same fluttering in the stomach, the same restlessness, the yawning. I keep on swallowing.

At other times it feels like being mildly drunk, or concussed. There is a sort of invisible blanket between the world and me. I find it hard to take in what anyone says. Or perhaps, hard to want to take it in. It is so uninteresting. Yet I want the others to be about me. I dread the moments when the house is empty. If only they would talk to one another and not to me....

Meanwhile, where is God? This is one of the most disquieting symptoms. When you are happy, so happy that you have no sense of needing Him, so happy that you are tempted to feel His claims upon you as an interruption, if you remember yourself and turn to Him with gratitude and praise, you will be—or so it feels—welcomed with open arms. But go to Him when your need is desperate, when all other help is vain, and what do you find? A door slammed in your face, and a sound of bolting and double bolting on the inside. After that, silence. You may as well turn away. The longer you wait, the more emphatic the silence will become. There are no lights in the windows. It might be an empty house. Was it ever inhabited? It seemed so once. And that seeming was as strong as this. What can this mean? Why is He so present a commander in our time of prosperity and so very absent a help in time of trouble?

I tried to put some of these thoughts to C. this afternoon. He reminded me that the same thing seems to have happened to Christ:

*It is helpful for everyone to read the Devotional and Scripture Readings and do the My Life with God Exercise before the meeting. Begin the meeting with silent prayer, then move directly to Reflecting on My Life with God below.*

'Why hast thou forsaken me?' I know. Does that make it easier to understand?

Not that I am (I think) in much danger of ceasing to believe in God. The real danger is of coming to believe such dreadful things about Him. The conclusion I dread is not, 'So there's no God after all,' but, 'So this is what God's really like. Deceive yourself no longer.'

Our elders submitted and said, 'Thy will be done.' How often had bitter resentment been stifled through sheer terror and an act of love—yes, in every sense, an act—put on to hide the operation?

Of course, it's easy to say that God seems absent at our greatest need because He *is* absent—non-existent. But then why does He seem so present when, to put it quite frankly, we don't ask for Him?[1]

## MY LIFE WITH GOD EXERCISE

We often take God's presence for granted until, as C. S. Lewis describes so eloquently, we reach the lowest point in our lives and no longer feel that he is there, for surely he would never allow such things to happen, never allow us to suffer so. When we are surrounded by the shroud of grief, the cloak of disappointment, the straitjacket of lost hope, the presence of God in our lives can seem to disappear into thin air like frost dissipates in the hot sun. With David we cry, "Deliver me, O my God!" from our feelings of being forsaken (Ps 3:7). The lover of our soul seems to be absent from every aspect of our life—our relations with other people, our job, our family, everything, even our own soul. During good times we very seldom ask, "Where is God?" But it is *the* question that haunts almost all of us when tragedy dogs our heels. It was the same for people we meet in the Bible: Job, David, Jeremiah, Jonah. No matter how hard they tried, or we try, we all doubt God's presence at times. We wonder if he is real or if our life is no more than "mist that is chased by the rays of the sun and overcome by its heat" (Wisdom of Solomon 2:4). So the other question that we as Christians must wrestle with during these times is, "How do I sense God in the midst of my doubt?"

Before the next meeting, try to set aside time each day to meditate in turn on each of the following Scriptures. Work through them in order. For some of the shorter passages, try writing the verses on a 3x5 card and tucking it in your bag or pocket so you can read it several times during the day. You might even write on the back of the card your insights into the Scripture. When you reach the passage from Romans, try to memorize verses 38–39.

Psalm 22:1–5 *my God, my God, why have you forsaken*
Psalm 31:1–10 *In You I take refuge, come quickly to my rescue.*
Hebrews 10:32–38a *But my righteous one will live by faith*
Romans 8:31–39 *If God for us who can be against us who will separate us — more than conquerors*
Job 19:1–27 *though I cry "I've been wronged" I get no response. I know my redeemer lives*

If you are going through a trying time, it may be best to consider the first two Scriptures in private, because they may elicit strong feelings. It is okay to be truthful with God and to pour out your heart about your feelings of abandonment.

*Can you describe a time when you felt God was absent from your life? How did you overcome that feeling, if you were able to? What insight, if any, did the Scripture passages offer?* *Many times — For the love of God compels me — Quitting is easy way out.*

**REFLECTING ON MY LIFE WITH GOD**
Allow each member a few moments to answer this question.

▶ **SCRIPTURE READING:** JOSHUA 2:1–15; 6:16B, 17, 23A, 25A

Then Joshua son of Nun sent two men secretly from Shittim as spies, saying, "Go, view the land, especially Jericho." So they went, and entered the house of a prostitute whose name was Rahab, and spent the night there. The king of Jericho was told, "Some Israelites have come here tonight to search out the land." Then the king of Jericho sent orders to Rahab, "Bring out the men who have come to you, who entered your house, for they have come only to search out the whole land." But the woman took the two men and hid them. Then she said, "True, the men came to me, but I did not know where they came from. And when it was time to close the gate at dark, the men went out. Where the men went I do not know. Pursue them quickly, for you can overtake them." She had, however, brought them up to the roof and hidden them with the stalks of flax that she had laid out on the roof. So the men pursued them on the way to the Jordan, as far as the fords. As soon as the pursuers had gone out, the gate was shut.

Before they went to sleep, she came up to them on the roof and said to the men: "I know that the LORD has given you the land, and that dread of you has fallen on us, and that all the inhabitants of the land melt in

After everyone has had a chance to respond to the question, ask a member to read this passage from Scripture.

fear before you. For we have heard how the LORD dried up the water of the Red Sea before you when you came out of Egypt, and what you did to the two kings of the Amorites that were beyond the Jordan, to Sihon and Og, whom you utterly destroyed. As soon as we heard it, our hearts melted, and there was no courage left in any of us because of you. The LORD your God is indeed God in heaven above and on earth below. Now then, since I have dealt kindly with you, swear to me by the LORD that you in turn will deal kindly with my family. Give me a sign of good faith that you will spare my father and mother, my brothers and sisters, and all who belong to them, and deliver our lives from death." The men said to her, "Our life for yours! If you do not tell this business of ours, then we will deal kindly and faithfully with you when the LORD gives us this land."

Then she let them down by a rope through the window, for her house was on the outer side of the city wall and she resided within the wall itself. . . .

Joshua said to the people . . . , "The city and all that is in it shall be devoted to the LORD for destruction. Only Rahab the prostitute and all who are with her in her house shall live because she hid the messengers we sent." . . . So the young men who had been spies went in and brought Rahab out, along with her father, her mother, her brothers, and all who belonged to her. . . . But Rahab the prostitute, with her family and all who belonged to her, Joshua spared.

REFLECTION QUESTION
Allow each person a few moments to respond to this question.

*How have you sensed God's presence in your life? Did you sense God before you became a Christian?* Yes - I believe, help my unbelief.

After a brief discussion, choose one person to read this section.

## ▶▶ GETTING THE PICTURE

The Scripture about Rahab comes at the end of the Israelites' forty-year odyssey in the wilderness, as they were preparing to invade Canaan. This story begins with the exodus of the Children of Israel from their enslavement to the Egyptian pharaoh. After long years of slavery, God hears the "groaning of the Israelites" and sends a reluctant Moses to convince the pharaoh to let the Israelites leave (Exod 2:23–24a; 3; 5). The Israelites leave Egypt in triumph, but it isn't long before they start grumbling about the hardships of the trip across the desert. Although

God is visibly present as a pillar of cloud by day and of fire by night, they rebel by worshipping a golden calf. After Moses makes amends to God for the people's behavior, God renews the covenant he had made with the children of Jacob.

But the Israelites rebel again when they reach the border of the land promised to Jacob, and ten of the Israelite spies report back that the land is too well defended for them to enter. Consequently, everyone who participated in the rebellion is left to wander in the wilderness until they die. Because Moses also disobeyed God, God forbids him to enter Canaan, and the mantle of leadership passes from Moses to Joshua. In the Scripture Reading, the Israelites are finally ready to enter the long-awaited Promised Land. Joshua sends the two spies ahead, and they have their encounter with Rahab.

Rahab is an unlikely candidate for a starring role in the drama of the Israelites. She is a prostitute, her marginality in her own society underscored by the place where she makes her home—at the very edge of Jericho, in the wall. Rahab lives in a culture that worships a multitude of localized gods intimately connected with nature, but she, along with the rest of the Canaanites, has heard stories about the God of the Israelites, a mobile God who travels with them, guiding them and performing miracles on the way. Through these stories and through the two spies who stay at her inn, Rahab is able to sense God, leading her to confess her faith in him and save the lives of the two men.

## ▶▶▶ GOING DEEPER

At first glance, the stories of Rahab and Lewis seem to have very little in common. Certainly the two were at very different places in their faith. Yet both eventually realized that God is present with us *all the time*, even when we don't feel his presence or understand his will, even when we don't truly know him.

Their stories make clear that people experience God's presence in different ways, according to their situation and the place where they are in their faith journey. Rahab was just beginning to know God. Her sense of God came only from what she had heard about God and what he had done. As far as we know, there was no intimate connection there, no relationship that helped her know that the God of the Israelites was the one true God. The people around her were afraid, yet it

*Have another member read this section.*

was still a huge risk for her to throw in her lot with these wandering Israelites. Jericho was a venerable old city with its own gods and virtually impregnable walls, as well she knew, since her own dwelling sat in the thick wall. The only reason for her to say and do what she did was that she believed in the God of the Israelites. Lewis, on the other hand, was already a well-known Christian. His writings and radio addresses touched the lives of millions. Yet he was not immune to suffering and pain, even doubt. After his wife died, God's presence seemed unsure for the first time since he came to Christ. His normally acute sense of God's presence had been dulled by the emotional pain he was going through. How cruel it seemed to him that, just at the time when he sorely needed God, the presence he had before taken for granted no longer seemed accessible.

In the beginning of our faith journey, our sense of God is often instinctual, as it was for Rahab. Rahab not only sensed the dread and fear of the inhabitants of Jericho but also the presence of God there with the two spies. She believed that the two spies would honor their promise after she had saved their lives. She may have lied to the king about the whereabouts of the Israelites for a number of reasons: to preserve herself and her family, to settle old scores, to start a new life, or simply to be on the winning side. Whatever the reason, her spirit was clearly sensitive to the call of God, and she believed in him. Consequently, she and her family were the only ones saved in all of Jericho. In contrast to Rahab's instinctive knowledge of God, at some points in our faith journey we may have to work to feel God's presence. Lewis was another sensitive soul, so accustomed to being able to feel God's presence, even when he did not ask, that the sudden failure to sense God's presence in his greatest need was all the more stark. As Chad Walsh wrote in the afterword to *A Grief Observed*, "His religion, which had seemed so sturdily based, began to crumble.... But as [*A Grief Observed*] comes to an end, the reader finds himself sharing the first timid movement of Lewis back toward a world that makes sense."[2] Through writing and prayer, Lewis worked to return to his sense of God's presence, searching for God in the midst of his emotional pain. Deep in his heart he sensed that God was present; it just took time and work to heal the hurt.

Sensing and honoring God's presence requires us to take risks or make difficult choices at times, as did both Rahab and Lewis. Rahab acknowledged that the Israelites' God was Lord of the universe and took action; Lewis wrote that he wondered where God was during his pain. By discarding the Canaanite gods and throwing her lot in with the Israelites

CONNECTING WITH GOD

and their God, Rahab risked the wrath of her fellow citizens. She also risked death if the spies did not honor their promise. In spite of her limited knowledge and sense of God's presence, Rahab took action based on her belief and made her bargain with the spies. As a result of her bravery, she is listed as one of Jesus's ancestors and is honored with a place in the "Faith Hall of Fame": "By faith Rahab the prostitute did not perish with those who were disobedient, because she had received the spies in peace" (Heb 11:31). Likewise, Lewis must have known he was taking an incredible personal and public risk in even writing down the frank questions and doubts he was feeling. He was so well known for his speaking and writing about the Christian life in England that had it been known that he was asking the question, "Where is God?" it could have put others' faith in jeopardy, could have been seen as a denial of his influential earlier writings. His honest search for God led him to conclude, however, that God is present with us even when we can't feel him.

*At what times in your life have you felt God's presence the most? The least?*

REFLECTION QUESTION
Allow each person a few moments to respond.

## ▶▶▶▶ POINTING TO GOD

As the story of Rahab teaches us, anyone can sense God's presence, no matter how far they may appear to be from God. This principle is also illustrated by an experience of writer Anne Lamott. Lamott's first experience of Jesus took place at perhaps the lowest point of her life: she had just had an abortion and had been drinking heavily and taking pills for a week. She started bleeding but was too ashamed by her drinking to call a friend or a doctor, so she lay down in the dark to sleep.

Choose one member to read this section.

> After a while, as I lay there, I became aware of someone with me, hunkered down in the corner, and I just assumed it was my father, whose presence I had felt over the years when I was frightened and alone. The feeling was so strong that I actually turned on the light for a moment to make sure no one was there—of course, there wasn't. But after a while, in the dark again, I knew beyond any doubt that it was Jesus. I felt him as surely as I feel my dog lying nearby as I write this.
>
> And I was appalled. I thought about my life and my brilliant hilarious progressive friends, I thought about what everyone

would think of me if I became a Christian, and it seemed an utterly impossible thing that simply could not be allowed to happen. I turned to the wall and said out loud, "I would rather die."

I felt him just sitting there on his haunches in the corner of my sleeping loft, watching me with patience and love, and I squinched my eyes shut, but that didn't help because that's not what I was seeing him with.

Finally, I fell asleep, and in the morning, he was gone.[3]

For days she felt that a cat was following her, wanting her to pick it up and welcome it into her home. But she was reluctant to do so because she knew that once she let "the cat" in, it would stay forever. After a week, she attended a nearby church, and after the service, she finally "took a long deep breath and said out loud, 'All right. You can come in.'"[4]

## ⮞⮞⮞⮞⮞ GOING FORWARD

✍ Have another person read this section.

God is present with all of us, regardless of our background or spiritual credentials. The greatest of us can doubt; the least of us can sense him. But whether we can feel him or not, "I am with you always, to the end of the age," Jesus tells us (Matt 28:20b). His promise to us is not that we will never suffer, but that we will never be alone. Often a sense of this presence like what Rahab and Anne Lamott experienced is the first step in our conversation with him. At other times, it is the first thing to leave us when we are in the midst of great pain, as was Lewis.

But Lewis worked hard to find a renewed sense of God's presence. Eventually he worked back to being able to praise God for the wonderful gift of his wife, and thus experienced a sense of his wife's presence as well as God's presence: "Don't we in praise somehow enjoy what we praise, however far we are from it? . . . [B]y praising I can still, in some degree, enjoy her, and already, in some degree, enjoy Him."[5] As Catherine Marshall and Frank Laubach attested in previous chapters, praising God continually, even for those things that don't seem like blessings, is a sure way to attune ourselves to God's presence.

**REFLECTION QUESTION**
Again, allow each member a few moments to answer this question.

*What might it be like if you sought to sense God's presence while doing your daily tasks, working, washing dishes, taking a shower? How might this change your life? What might you do more of, less of?*

Beloved Disciple

CONNECTING WITH GOD

This concludes our look at sensing God's presence. In the next chapter we will turn our attention to another avenue of communicating with God—encountering his messengers.

After everyone has had a chance to respond, the leader reads this paragraph.

## CLOSING PRAYER

To you, O LORD, I lift up my soul.
Make me to know your ways, O LORD;
    teach me your paths.
Lead me in your truth, and teach me,
    for you are the God of my salvation,
    for you I wait all day long.
"Come," my heart says, "seek his face!"
    Your face, LORD, do I seek.
Give ear to my words, O LORD;
    give heed to my sighing.
Listen to the sound of my cry,
    my King and my God,
    for to you I pray. Amen. (PSS 25:1, 4–5; 27:8; 5:1–2)

Allow some time for members to encourage one another to read the Devotional and Scripture Readings and do the exercise in the following chapter before the next meeting. Then invite the members to be silent for a few moments before leading them in reading the Closing Prayer aloud together.

At the end of the Closing Prayer, the leader asks for a volunteer to lead the next meeting.

## TAKING IT FURTHER

Brother Lawrence, a seventeenth-century Parisian monk, excelled at practicing the presence of God. In *The Practice of the Presence of God,* he wrote about establishing a sense of the presence of God at all times by continually talking to God and offering all actions to him. Try Brother Lawrence's method and practice the presence of God. Seek to pay attention to God while doing daily tasks—washing your face, sweeping, walking, cooking, reading. Try to be fully present in the moment, not thinking about what you're going to do in the next minute or next week, but just focusing on the present task and keeping up a conversation with God about what you are doing.

**ADDITIONAL EXERCISE**

Brother Lawrence. *The Practice of the Presence of God.* New Kensington, PA: Whitaker House, 1982.
de Caussade, Jean-Pierre. *The Sacrament of the Present Moment.* Translated by Kitty Muggeridge. San Francisco: HarperSanFrancisco, 1981.
Gresham, Douglas. *Lenten Lands.* San Francisco: HarperSanFrancisco, 1988.

**ADDITIONAL RESOURCES**

Lewis, C. S. *A Grief Observed*. San Francisco: HarperSanFrancisco, 1961.

Yancey, Philip. *Disappointment with God*. Grand Rapids, MI: Zondervan, 1997.

**ADDITIONAL REFLECTION QUESTIONS**

*Whose experience do you relate to more easily, Rahab's, Lewis's, or Lamott's? Why?*

*Do you see yourself as a person who intuits God's presence more easily than others? In what ways is that helpful? In what ways might it be a problem?*

*What does sensing God's presence mean to you? Is it an understanding or knowledge of him, a whisper on the back of your neck, an intuition, a feeling—all or none of these?*

a thought entering my head - a pressure on my body

# 10 ENCOUNTERING GOD'S MESSENGERS

## DEVOTIONAL READING

CORRIE TEN BOOM, *The Hiding Place*

It was what my leaping heart had told me: a Bible, the entire Book in a compact volume, tucked inside a small pouch with a string for wearing around the neck as we had once carried our identity cards. I dropped it quickly over my head and down my back beneath my blouse....

"*Ravensbruck!*"

Like a whispered curse, the word passed back through the line. This was the notorious women's death camp itself, the very symbol to Dutch hearts of all that was evil. As we stumbled down the hill, I felt the little Bible bumping on my back. As long as we had that, I thought, we could face even hell itself. But how could we conceal it through the inspection I knew lay ahead?...

As each woman reached a desk where some officers sat she had to lay her blanket, pillowcase, and whatever else she carried onto a growing pile of these things. A few desks further along she had to strip off every scrap of clothes, throw them onto a second pile, and walk naked past the scrutiny of a dozen S.S. men into the shower room. Coming out of the shower she wore only a thin prison dress and a pair of shoes.... [W]e needed our Bible.

Timidly Betsie and I stepped out of line and walked to the door of the big, dank-smelling room with its row on row of overhead spigots.... [S]tacked in the far corner, a pile of old wooden benches.... [I]n an instant I had wrapped [the sweater] around the Bible and the vitamin bottle and stuffed the precious bundle behind the benches....

Of course when I put on the flimsy prison dress, the Bible bulged beneath it. But that was His business, not mine. At the exit, guards were feeling every prisoner, front, back, and sides. I prayed, "Oh, Lord, send your angels to surround us." But then I remembered that angels are spirits

*It is helpful for everyone to read the Devotional and Scripture Readings and do the My Life with God Exercise before the meeting. Begin the meeting with silent prayer, then move directly to Reflecting on My Life with God below.*

and you can see through them. What I needed was an angel to shield me so the guards could not see me. "Lord," I prayed again, "make your angels untransparent...."

The woman ahead of me was searched. Behind me, Betsie was searched. They did not touch or even look at me. It was as though I was blocked out of their sight.

Outside the building was a second ordeal, another line of guards examining each prisoner again. I slowed down as I reached them, but the captain shoved me roughly by the shoulder. "Move along! You're holding up the line."[1]

## MY LIFE WITH GOD EXERCISE

Even though almost all of us have heard some awe-inspiring story like Corrie ten Boom's about an encounter with angels, many Christians remain at best uncertain and at worst quite skeptical about angels and their place in the modern world. This is at least partly attributable to the prevalence of angel references in popular culture and New Age beliefs. All this hype has left many of us unclear as to what exactly the Bible has to say about such phenomena. Our exercise will shore up our knowledge about the biblical depiction of angels. The table below lists some passages in which angels appear. Please read as many of the passages as you can and attempt to fill in the rest of the material in the table. You won't be able to fill in every box for each reference, but fill in the ones you can.

| Scripture | Characteristics (name/appearance) | Task/Message | Person(s) Angel(s) appeared to | Reaction |
|---|---|---|---|---|
| Genesis 32:1–2 | Jacob – Angels of God met him | God is w/ you | Jacob | Jacob recognizes camp of God. |
| Exodus 3:1–4:17; Acts 7:30, 35 | flame of fire Angel appeared to Moses in bush | God speaking | Moses | Moses listens w/ reservations |
| Numbers 22:20–35 | Angel of Lord opposing | opposes/ blocking | Balaam | went back |
| Judges 6:11–24 | Angel of Lord | encouragement | Gideon | fleece |

CONNECTING WITH GOD

| Scripture | Characteristics (name/appearance) | Task/Message | Person(s) Angel(s) appeared to | Reaction |
|---|---|---|---|---|
| 2 Samuel 24:10–25; 1 Chronicles 21:7–30 | Angel of Destruction | to destroy Jerusalem | David | built an altar repentance/ remorse |
| 1 Kings 19:1–8 | Angel of succor | to give succor | Elijah | refreshed + strengthened |
| Daniel 3:19–30; Prayer of Azariah, 26–27 | 4th men | protect Shadrach, meshok... | All | faith – Awe |
| Daniel 6:16–23; Bel & the Dragon, 31–41 | | | | |
| Daniel 9:20–27 | | | | |
| Matthew 4:1–11 | Devil Angels of Comfort | tempt J.C give him ministrations | J. C | Word of God |
| Matthew 28:1–8; Luke 24:1–12; John 20:1–18 | | | | |
| Luke 1:26–38 | | | | |
| Luke 2:8–15 | | | | |
| Luke 22:39–46 | Angel of Strength | | J.C | he went on |
| Acts 5:17–21 | | | | |
| Acts 12:1–11 | Angel of rescue | rescue Peter from Prison | Peter | freed |

*How did you perceive angels before you read the story about Corrie ten Boom's experience and the biblical passages where they appear to humans? Afterward?*

*How do you perceive angels — experiences?*

## ➤ SCRIPTURE READING: LUKE 1:8, 11–20, 26–38

Once when [Zechariah] was serving as priest before God and his section was on duty . . . there appeared to him an angel of the Lord, standing at the right side of the altar of incense. When Zechariah saw him, he was terrified; and fear overwhelmed him. But the angel said to him, "Do not be afraid, Zechariah, for your prayer has been heard. Your wife Elizabeth will bear you a son, and you will name him John. You will have joy and gladness, and many will rejoice at his birth, for he will be great in the sight of the Lord. He must never drink wine or strong drink; even before his birth he will be filled with the Holy Spirit. He will turn many of the people of Israel to the Lord their God. With the spirit and power of Elijah he will go before him, to turn the hearts of parents to their children, and the disobedient to the wisdom of the righteous, to make ready a people prepared for the Lord." Zechariah said to the angel, "How will I know that this is so? For I am an old man, and my wife is getting on in years." The angel replied, "I am Gabriel. I stand in the presence of God, and I have been sent to speak to you and to bring you this good news. But now, because you did not believe my words, which will be fulfilled in their time, you will become mute, unable to speak, until the day these things occur. . . ."

In the sixth month the angel Gabriel was sent by God to a town in Galilee called Nazareth, to a virgin engaged to a man whose name was Joseph, of the house of David. The virgin's name was Mary. And he came to her and said, "Greetings, favored one! The Lord is with you." But she was much perplexed by his words and pondered what sort of greeting this might be. The angel said to her, "Do not be afraid, Mary, for you have found favor with God. And now, you will conceive in your womb and bear a son, and you will name him Jesus. He will be great, and will be called the Son of the Most High, and the Lord God will give to him the throne of his ancestor David. He will reign over the house of Jacob forever, and of his kingdom there will be no end." Mary said to the angel, "How can this be, since I am a virgin?" The angel said to her, "The Holy Spirit will come upon you, and the power of the Most High will overshadow you; therefore the child to be born will be holy; he will be called Son of God. And now, your relative Elizabeth in her old age has also conceived a son; and this is the sixth month for her who was said to be barren. For nothing will be impossible with God." Then Mary said, "Here am I, the servant of the Lord; let it be with me according to your word." Then the angel departed from her.

REFLECTION QUESTION
Allow each person a few moments to respond to this question.

*Compare Zechariah's reaction to the angel with Mary's reaction. If an angel were to come to you, would your reaction be closer to Zechariah's or Mary's? Why?*

Z didn't believe, May believed but couldn't see how. Don't know how. I think like Mary or maybe like Sarai - laugh.

## ▶▶ GETTING THE PICTURE

Our first Scripture describes the angel Gabriel's appearance in the Temple to Zechariah, the father of John the Baptist. Zechariah's service in the Temple that day was likely one of the high points of his life. A descendant of Levi, Zechariah was a member of the priestly class that served as an intermediary between God and the people of Israel in the Herodian Temple of Zechariah's time. During his lifetime, there were more priests than positions, so they were divided into twenty-four groups or sections. Each section served in the Temple for one week twice a year and at major festivals.

After a brief discussion, choose one person to read this section.

The focus of the Temple was the Holy of Holies and the Holy Place. The Holy of Holies, where the ark of the covenant was originally placed, was entered only once a year, by the high priest on the Day of Atonement. The Holy Place, in front of the Holy of Holies, contained a lamp stand, the bread of the Presence with its table, and the altar of incense, all of which required regular care. In the Herodian Temple, because there were so many priests, they were chosen by lot to preside at the offering of the incense and replenish the oil in the lamps. This was probably a once-in-a-lifetime opportunity for each priest. At this high point of Zechariah's life, Gabriel appears to him.

Our second Scripture is the story of Gabriel's appearance to Mary, the mother of Jesus. The contrast between the two stories is striking. First, we don't know the names of Mary's forebears because Israelites traced their ancestry through the male line. The lineage of Jesus's adoptive father, Joseph, through King David is given but not Mary's (see Matt 1:1–16 and Luke 3:23–38). However, we know that in ancient cultures, as in contemporary agrarian societies, extended families often lived in the same general area, so it is very possible that Mary was a relative of Joseph and could also claim David as an ancestor.

Second, we know that Mary, unlike Zechariah, was quite young, because she was engaged but not yet married. The custom in the first century was for young girls to be engaged soon after puberty but not to have sexual intercourse with their fiancés until they were married. Thus Joseph planned to "dismiss her quietly" when he found out that Mary had become pregnant prior to their marriage (Matt 1:18–19). Third, it is clear that Mary had very little or no social standing even though her relatives Zechariah and Elizabeth belonged to a much-admired social class, because Joseph and Mary offered "a pair of turtledoves or two young pigeons" as a sacrifice at the Temple in Jerusalem when they presented Jesus (Luke 2:22–24). The Mosaic law specified that a woman who had recently given birth and couldn't afford a sheep to sacrifice during the purification rite could instead sacrifice two turtledoves or pigeons (Lev 12). Hence Joseph and Mary must have been poor, and then as today, poor people belonged to the lowest rung of society.

## ▶▶▶ GOING DEEPER

✍ Have another member read this section.

In this scientific age it can be difficult to believe in the existence of beings that have no physical form we can touch or measure and who come and go without leaving any trace of their presence. But it is equally hard to discount the existence of angels when we read stories like Corrie ten Boom's and the Scripture passages cited above. As we discussed in earlier chapters, we have no reason not to believe that all of the ways God spoke to his people in the Bible are still possible today.

There are several principles of spiritual formation we can learn from the angel stories in the Devotional and Scripture Readings. First, God is always working for our good. Because Corrie ten Boom escaped being searched, a Bible was preserved that she could use not only for her own spiritual nourishment but for the encouragement of her sister and the other prisoners. The angel Gabriel brought good news to Elizabeth and Zechariah, who had waited for decades to have a child. Though Gabriel's message to Mary carried some immediate social complications for her as an individual, it was news that she and the children of Israel had anticipated for centuries. It was good news for Mary and for all humankind.

These stories remind us that even in the midst of less than ideal circumstances, God cares for us enough to protect us and encourage us, and

CONNECTING WITH GOD

if necessary, he will use supernatural means to do so. *The Hiding Place* is full of stories about how the ten Booms survived in Ravensbruck because God sent special people, including angels, into their lives. Elizabeth's pregnancy removed the humiliation of barrenness from her life. In the midst of Mary's pregnancy, God provided a husband, Joseph, to care for her and to take her and Jesus to Egypt when Herod became a threat to their well-being.

*But not her sister Betsie*

We also learn that God hears our prayers, simple though they may be. Corrie ten Boom's prayer was answered immediately because it furthered the kingdom of God. In the case of Elizabeth and Zechariah, it wasn't in the best interests of the kingdom for God to answer them instantly, but they were answered when the time was right.

Finally, as we saw in the chapter on dreams and visions, although we certainly have no control over whether God honors us with a message or visit from an angel, how we respond to that kind of experience is important and quite telling of the condition of our hearts. Though the questions Zechariah and Mary asked the angel were similar, Scripture tells us that their internal reactions were quite different. When Zechariah saw the angel, he was "terrified; and fear overwhelmed him," whereas Mary was "perplexed by [Gabriel's] words and pondered" his greeting. These different reactions make us wonder if Zechariah's heart was guarded or skeptical about what the Lord could do. His age and position might have influenced him to become perfunctory and jaded in his approach to God. As a result of his doubt, Zechariah was silenced until the birth of his son. Mary's response indicates a heart that is open and expectant; she had not yet had time to view her relationship with God as just another duty in a life full of obligations. In sharp contrast to Zechariah's forced silence, Mary's encounter with the angel ends with a powerful statement of acquiescence: "Here am I, the servant of the Lord; let it be with me according to your word."

*Have you ever experienced an angelic visitation or known someone who has? What kind of role do you think angels play in today's world?*

Bea's Brother   Boss' sister Karen

**REFLECTION QUESTION**
Allow each person a few moments to respond.

## ▶▶▶▶ POINTING TO GOD

John G. Paton, a Scot, served as a missionary in the New Hebrides Islands in the mid-nineteenth century. One night hostile natives surrounded the

✍ Choose one member to read this section.

mission building where Paton and his wife lived, intending to burn the place down and kill the Patons. The couple prayed all night for God to deliver them, and when morning finally came their prayers were answered. Surprisingly, the attackers had left without any reason that the couple could discern. A year later, one of the men who had threatened them, the chief of a local tribe, converted to Christianity. Rev. Paton asked him why they hadn't burned down the house that night and killed him and his wife. The man replied, "Who were all those men you had with you there?" Paton responded that there had been no men, just him and his wife. The chief then said that they had seen hundreds of large men wearing shining clothes and holding drawn swords standing guard around the mission. The chief and his men had been too afraid to attack a building with such defenses. Only then did Paton believe that angels had protected him and his wife that night.[2] This story is a wonderful illustration of the question the writer of Hebrews asks: "Are not all angels spirits in the divine service, sent to serve for the sake of those who are to inherit salvation?" (1:14).

## ▶▶▶▶▶ GOING FORWARD

Have another person read this section.

Psalm 91:11 states, "For he will command his angels concerning you to guard you in all your ways." The stories of the Patons, Corrie ten Boom, Zechariah, and Mary all attest to that fact. God hears our prayers, and he answers them in many ways, including the use of angels to guide us and protect us. In addition, we learned from the Scriptures we studied that many times God sends angels to deliver messages and guidance when we least expect it. The appearance of angels in our lives is controlled by God, not us. Thus it is a mistake to place too much emphasis on angels, venerating and even (perhaps unintentionally) honoring them above God. Angels point always to God; they serve at his pleasure, carrying his messages, heralding his presence, and carrying out his will.

As we learn lessons about God from his creation, Scripture, and our relationships with those around us, we can also learn important lessons about God from the angels who carry out his wishes for the creation—namely, that God works in the world around us, that he hears our prayers and answers them according to his will, and that the intentions of our hearts matter a great deal.

➤ *What else do angels teach us about God?* He hears us, there are other create beings besides us — God works in mysterious ways

**REFLECTION QUESTION**
Again, allow each member a few moments to answer this question.

This concludes our look at encountering God's messengers. In the next chapter we will turn our attention to another avenue of connecting with God—wrestling with him.

➷ After everyone has had a chance to respond, the leader reads this paragraph.

## CLOSING PRAYER

To you, O Lord, I lift up my soul.
Make me to know your ways, O Lord;
> teach me your paths.
Lead me in your truth, and teach me,
> for you are the God of my salvation,
> for you I wait all day long.
"Come," my heart says, "seek his face!"
> Your face, Lord, do I seek.
Give ear to my words, O Lord;
> give heed to my sighing.
Listen to the sound of my cry,
> my King and my God,
> for to you I pray. Amen. (PSS 25:1, 4–5; 27:8; 5:1–2)

➷ **Allow some time for members to encourage one another to read the Devotional and Scripture Readings and do the exercise in the following chapter before the next meeting.** Then invite the members to be silent for a few moments before leading them in reading the Closing Prayer aloud together.

➷ At the end of the Closing Prayer, the leader asks for a volunteer to lead the next meeting.

## TAKING IT FURTHER

Do some angel research alone or with friends. Search the Internet and check out some of the Web sites about angels. Watch some angel movies, such as *City of Angels* or *It's a Wonderful Life,* or a TV program like *Touched by an Angel.* What kind of attitude toward angels do you see? What would you agree or disagree with after studying some of the Scriptures that mention visits from angels?

**ADDITIONAL EXERCISE**
Try doing this exercise at an additional meeting of your group.

Graham, Billy. *Angels: God's Secret Agents.* Nashville, TN: W Publishing Group, 1995.
Spangler, Ann. *An Angel a Day.* Grand Rapids, MI: Zondervan, 1994.
Ten Boom, Corrie. *Tramp for the Lord.* Old Tappan, NJ: Christian Literature Crusade & Revell, 1974.

**ADDITIONAL RESOURCES**

What lessons did you learn about God from studying the biblical record of encounters with angels?

None — I had already known

Are there times when we should pray specifically for the assistance of an angel, as Corrie ten Boom did in the Devotional Reading? Explain. If so, what might some be?

? I don't but maybe should

What would you correct about today's mainstream view of angels?

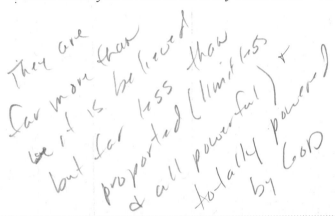

They are far more than we it is believed but far less than proported (limitless) & all powerful) totally powered by GOD

# 11

# WRESTLING WITH GOD

KEY SCRIPTURE: Genesis 18:1–5, 16–33

## DEVOTIONAL READING

BILLY GRAHAM, *Just As I Am*

When the moment came to walk to the pulpit in the tiny Bostwick Baptist Church, my knees shook and perspiration glistened on my hands. I launched into sermon number one. It seemed to be over almost as soon as I got started, so I added number two. And number three. And eventually number four. Then I sat down.

Eight minutes—that was all it took to preach all four of my sermons! Was this the stuff of which those marvelous preachers at Florida Bible Institute were made?

Believe it or not, though, when I got back to campus I felt that I had grown spiritually through the experience. But at the same time I was concerned: I could not get away from a nagging feeling in my heart that I was being called by God to preach the Gospel. I did not welcome that call....

Despite my awkward debut in Bostwick at Easter, Dr. Minder invited me to speak to his Sunday night youth group at the Tampa Gospel Tabernacle. Then came the moment when he asked me to preach at a regular service. I was downright frightened....

When I returned to the Institute after summer vacation that first year, I little guessed that I would face my severest test before the school year was over, when a beautiful girl complicated my life.... That woeful night in the spring of 1938 when she called it quits between us was Paradise Lost for me.... But my problem was deeper than losing a girlfriend, and in my heart I admitted it. The issue was not trying to do something to please her and win her back.... The issue was doing what pleased the Lord. If I refused that, could I expect the future to hold any happiness?

*It is helpful for everyone to read the Devotional and Scripture Readings and do the My Life with God Exercise before the meeting. Begin the meeting with silent prayer, then move directly to Reflecting on My Life with God below.*

For some weeks, triggered by a profoundly searching sermon in chapel, I paced those deserted, echoing streets of Temple Terrace.... I never felt so alone in my life—or so close to God. I walked through the late-night hours, struggling with the Holy Spirit over the call of God to be a minister. That was the last thing I wanted to be, and I had used all kinds of rationalizations to convince God to let me do something else....

Many people responded to my preaching by confessing faith in Christ and being converted. My teachers and classmates seemed to affirm that this ministry was good and right for me. But did I want to preach for a lifetime? I asked myself that question for the umpteenth time on one of my nighttime walks around the golf course. The inner, irresistible urge would not subside. Finally, one night, I got down on my knees at the edge of one of the greens. Then I prostrated myself on the dewy turf. "O God," I sobbed, "if you want me to serve you, I will."[1]

## MY LIFE WITH GOD EXERCISE

To actively wrestle with God like Billy Graham did over his vocation may make us uncomfortable, but it is another way that we communicate individually with God. In Graham's case, like Moses, Jeremiah, and Jonah before him, he wrestled with God over a call that he eventually accepted. Although Graham was resisting God's will, what was important was that he continued to talk with God about it. Scripture shows us many other kinds of wrestling with God. Job and the psalmists lamented to God about things they did not understand in the world around them. Abraham negotiated with God over the fate of the cities of Sodom and Gomorrah. By persistently bringing matters before God, we can come to a better understanding of God and God's will.

As soon as you can, set aside a time to bring your life before the Holy Spirit to identify those times you wrestled with God over some decision or event in your life or one that impacted your family. It's also okay to include concerns about the needs of people outside your family, such as others' health, concerns about your church, community, or nation, or prayers for those in God's service in the kingdom, if such concerns come to mind. One way to make this reflection on your life more manageable is to divide it into periods, bringing them one at a time before the Holy Spirit. This may take some time, so be patient with yourself. Should you find that you have never brought anything repeatedly before God, quietly ask God to

CONNECTING WITH GOD

affirm with your spirit that it is okay to talk persistently and transparently with him until issues are resolved or your spirit finds peace.

At this point, it might help to write down those situations or circumstances in your life and the lives of others over which you intend to "wrestle" with God now and in the future. This exercise may take some thought outside of the time that you set apart to spend with God, so you may want to keep the piece of paper handy to write down items as you think of them. Don't be surprised if this exercise takes a good part of your daily time with God for several days. Many times the work of the Holy Spirit doesn't fit perfectly within our schedules.

*Teaching Job*

*What did you discover about your "wrestlings" as you did this exercise? Can you describe the nature of the specific events and circumstances you wrestled with God about? Personal circumstances? The health and welfare of others? Local, national, or international issues? Are you comfortable or uncomfortable with this type of communication with God? How does wrestling differ from other kinds of prayer?*

**REFLECTING ON MY LIFE WITH GOD**
Allow each member a few moments to answer this question.

▶ **SCRIPTURE READING:** GENESIS 18:1–5, 16–33

After everyone has had a chance to respond to the question, ask a member to read this passage from Scripture.

The LORD appeared to Abraham by the oaks of Mamre, as he sat at the entrance of his tent in the heat of the day. He looked up and saw three men standing near him. When he saw them, he ran from the tent entrance to meet them, and bowed down to the ground. He said, "My lord, if I find favor with you, do not pass by your servant. Let a little water be brought, and wash your feet, and rest yourselves under the tree. Let me bring a little bread, that you may refresh yourselves, and after that you may pass on—since you have come to your servant." So they said, "Do as you have said. . . ."

Then the men set out from there, and they looked toward Sodom; and Abraham went with them to set them on their way. The LORD said, "Shall I hide from Abraham what I am about to do, seeing that Abraham shall become a great and mighty nation, and all the nations of the earth shall be blessed in him? No, for I have chosen him, that he may charge his children and his household after him to keep the way of the LORD by doing righteousness and justice; so that the LORD may bring about for Abraham what he has promised him." Then the LORD said, "How great is the outcry against Sodom and Gomorrah and how very grave their sin! I must go down and see whether they have done altogether according to the outcry that has come to me; and if not, I will know."

So the men turned from there, and went toward Sodom, while Abraham remained standing before the LORD. Then Abraham came near and said, "Will you indeed sweep away the righteous with the wicked? Suppose there are fifty righteous within the city; will you then sweep away the place and not forgive it for the fifty righteous who are in it? Far be it from you to do such a thing, to slay the righteous with the wicked, so that the righteous fare as the wicked! Far be that from you! Shall not the Judge of all the earth do what is just?" And the LORD said, "If I find at Sodom fifty righteous in the city, I will forgive the whole place for their sake." Abraham answered, "Let me take it upon myself to speak to the Lord, I who am but dust and ashes. Suppose five of the fifty righteous are lacking? Will you destroy the whole city for lack of five?" And he said, "I will not destroy it if I find forty-five there." Again he spoke to him, "Suppose forty are found there." He answered, "For the sake of forty I will not do it." Then he said, "Oh do not let the Lord be angry if I speak. Suppose thirty are found there." He answered, "I will not do it, if I find thirty there." He said, "Let me take it upon myself to speak to the Lord. Suppose twenty are found there." He answered, "For the sake of twenty I will not destroy it." Then he said, "Oh do not let the Lord be angry if I speak just once more. Suppose ten are found there." He answered, "For the sake of ten I will not destroy it." And the LORD went his way, when he had finished speaking to Abraham; and Abraham returned to his place.

**REFLECTION QUESTION**
Allow each person a few moments to respond to this question.

*How did you react to Abraham's bargaining with God? Can you imagine approaching God in this way?* Bible says to go boldly also A. not asking for himself but others

After a brief discussion, choose one person to read this section.

## ▶▶ GETTING THE PICTURE

We first meet Abram as he moves from Ur, his birthplace, to Haran, along with his father Terah, his nephew Lot, and his wife Sarai. After Terah's death, the Lord says to Abram, "Go from your country and your kindred and your father's house to the land that I will show you" (Gen 12:1). Again, Abram, Sarai, and Lot move to Canaan along with all of their slaves and possessions. Abram's arrival in Canaan sets in motion a series of incidents that lead up to the appearance of the Lord and the men by the oaks of Mamre. A famine forces them to leave Canaan and go to Egypt in search of food. While there, Abram tells the pharaoh a half-lie about his relationship to Sarai. (He claims she is his sister when in truth she is his half-sister and wife.) This lie brings trouble to the pharaoh's household. From Egypt they journey in stages back to Bethel, where Lot apparently makes known his desire to part company with Abram because "the land could not support both of them living together . . . and there was strife between the herders of Abram's livestock and the herders of Lot's livestock" (13:6–7). Abram gives Lot his choice of the land, and he chooses to settle in Sodom, leaving Canaan to Abram. After Lot leaves, the Lord again speaks to Abram, telling him that the land as far as he can see will belong to him and his descendants forever and that they will be as numerous as "the dust of the earth.... So Abram moved his tent, and came and settled by the oaks of Mamre" (vv 16–18).

Here the Lord appears again to Abram and promises that he will produce an heir, that he and his descendants will possess the land of Canaan, and that he will have a long life. In spite of the Lord's promise to provide an heir, Sarai becomes impatient and, following the custom of the day, gives her Egyptian slave-girl, Hagar, to Abram as a wife. Abram is eighty-six years old when Hagar bears a son, Ishmael.

When Abram is ninety-nine, the Lord appears to him again. He changes Abram's name to Abraham and Sarai's name to Sarah. This time God makes a covenant with Abraham in which he promises Abraham an heir, descendants as numerous as the stars, and the land of Canaan. As a sign of the covenant, Abraham "circumcised the flesh" of the foreskins of every male in his household, including all of his slaves and Ishmael, "as God had said to him" (17:23–27). The Scripture Reading immediately follows the circumcision, a sign of Abraham's covenant with God.

## ▶▶▶ GOING DEEPER

Abraham and Billy Graham wrestled with God in different ways. Abraham wrestled with the Lord over the fate of two cities and their inhabitants; Graham wrestled with the Holy Spirit over what he believed God was calling him to do. Abraham's verbal struggle with the Lord affected the lives of the inhabitants of Sodom and Gomorrah and the future of his nephew, Lot, and his family; Graham's internal wrestling impacted his own life and, eventually, the spiritual life of millions of other people.

🖅 Have another member read this section.

The most noticeable thing about Abraham's confrontation with the Lord and Graham's dialogue with the Holy Spirit is that they are both based on a reverent friendship with God. At the appearance of the three men, Abraham, as great a man as he was, shows deference to them by bowing, making them comfortable, and serving them food. Then, during his dialogue with the Lord over the fate of Sodom and Gomorrah, Abraham's words are calm and measured, as our words should be when we disagree with a friend. They also show humility: "Let me take it upon myself to speak to the Lord, I who am but dust and ashes" (v 27). Similarly, Graham knows God well; he is accustomed to engaging in long conversations with him. He wants to obey God, but he hopes that God's will is not what he is starting to suspect—that he become a minister. Finally, he humbly acquiesces to God's will with his prayer, "O God, if you want me to serve you, I will."

In addition, we learn that God initiates and in a sense invites us to wrestle with him over issues that affect our lives and the lives of those we care about. In Genesis 18:20, the Lord told Abraham where he was going and for what reason. When the Lord lingered behind, that gave Abraham a chance to make his case for not destroying everyone in the cities. Billy Graham wrestled with the nudging of the Holy Spirit as he was trying to make a decision about his life's vocation. Both doors were opened by God.

Finally, it is important to be persistent in bringing our question or request before the Lord. Among Jesus's many teachings is the parable of the Widow and Unjust Judge (Luke 18:2–5). Just as the judge responded to the widow's persistent pleas for justice, so should we expect God to respond to our pleas, even if the answer, as in Graham's case, is not what we want. As a result of his reverent friendship with God, Abraham was persistent in asking God for fifty righteous people, then for forty-five, then for forty, and so on until they both arrived at the final figure, which would save Sodom and Gomorrah from imminent destruction. Similarly, Graham was persistent in talking with God about the decision the Holy Spirit was leading him to make. The decision didn't come easily, but afterward Graham felt settled in his choice.

These stories confirm that if we are brave enough to bring our concerns before God, we will receive guidance from him. Probably none of us will have an encounter with the Lord similar to Abraham's, but we must remember that God is in the business of communicating with us; it is our task to prepare and open our hearts so that we can hear his messages. Once Graham and Abraham opened their hearts enough to talk

CONNECTING WITH GOD

honestly with God, he was able to use their questions and struggles to bring them to greater faith.

*Which kind of wrestling with God do you find yourself engaging in more— Billy Graham's wrestling over God's will for his life or Abraham's struggle over God's role in the world?*

**REFLECTION QUESTION**
Allow each person a few moments to respond.

## ▶▶▶ POINTING TO GOD

One of the most common things people wrestle with God about is sickness and death, both their own and that of others. John Donne, the noted seventeenth-century British poet and writer, was no exception to this rule. Throughout his life difficult setbacks alternated with great successes. He struggled vocationally for many years. As a young man, he secretly married Ann More. Since she was underage, the marriage was illegal, and when Ann's father learned of it, he had Donne thrown into prison and dismissed from his prestigious job as a secretary to Sir Thomas Egerton.[2] Having grown accustomed to poverty and after various other setbacks, Donne turned to the church in desperation and was ordained as an Anglican priest in 1615.[3] He experienced immediate success. Shortly after his ordination Donne was appointed Chaplain-in-Ordinary to King James I.[4] He also preached outside the court, and his eloquence led to his becoming known as perhaps the greatest preacher of the seventeenth century. After suffering the loss of his wife in 1617, in 1621 he received his greatest appointment, that of Dean of St. Paul's Cathedral in London.

Yet only two years after his appointment Donne became very ill. He was diagnosed with bubonic plague, although the illness was later determined to be a form of typhus. Confined to his bed, Donne wrote *Devotions,* in which he wrestled with God over his confusion about his illness. Why now, just when he was in a position to be of real service to God? His writings became more and more despondent. "O who, if before hee had a beeing, he could have sense of this miserie, would buy a being here upon these conditions?" he wrote.[5] But his meditations took a sharp turn when he heard church bells ringing outside his window. Donne's first thought was that his friends had rung the bells for him, in anticipation of his death, but then he realized that they were ringing

✒ Choose one member to read this section.

because his neighbor had died of the plague. This bell-ringing moment became an awakening for him. Not only were other people suffering and even dying around him, he started to ask himself if he was ready to meet God. His prayers and writings, which had before asked God to take away his pain, now started to ask for his pain to be redeemed, transformed. For he realized that those times in his life when he had suffered the most had been the times when he had experienced the most spiritual growth. He penned some of his most famous lines about his insight:

> No man is an island, entire of itself; every man is a piece of the continent, a part of the main. If a clod be washed away by the sea, Europe is the less, as well as if a promontory were, as well as if a manor of thy friend's or of thine own were: any man's death diminishes me, because I am involved in mankind, and therefore never send to know for whom the bell tolls; it tolls for thee. Neither can we call this a begging of misery, or a borrowing of misery, as though we were not miserable enough of ourselves, but must fetch in more from the next house, in taking upon us the misery of our neighbours. Truly it were an excusable covetousness if we did, for affliction is a treasure, and scarce any man hath enough of it, No man hath affliction enough that is not matured and ripened by it, and made fit for God by that affliction.[6]

Donne spent the rest of his illness, from which he did recover, working to turn his mind from himself to others, devoting himself to Spiritual Disciplines such as prayer, meditation, and confession. His honest wrestling with God had led him to an insight about the meaning of life, death, and suffering—insight that his influential writings have passed on to countless others.

## ▶▶▶▶ GOING FORWARD

*Have another person read this section.*

The Bible makes clear that God desires open and frank communication with us. We may claim we have no secrets from God, but sometimes it is difficult to engage him openly about things we cannot understand or areas where we disagree with him. Some of us feel that it is inappropriate or irreverent to admit that we have such disagreements or questions. Yet if we have doubts and concerns and we don't bring them to him, how can we expect change or understanding? From Abraham to the psalmists to contemporary Christians like Billy Graham, we see people who struggled with God and emerged with stronger faith and a closer relationship with God. God is not afraid of our dark thoughts and is patient with our questions and the gaps in our understanding. Only when we turn to him, struggle with him, can he teach us.

*Looking back, what are some issues that you should have brought before God and didn't? Why didn't you?*

REFLECTION QUESTION
Again, allow each member a few moments to answer this question.

This concludes our look at wrestling with God. In the next chapter we will turn our attention to another avenue of communicating with God—walking with him.

🖙 After everyone has had a chance to respond, the leader reads this paragraph.

## CLOSING PRAYER

To you, O LORD, I lift up my soul.
Make me to know your ways, O LORD;
    teach me your paths.
Lead me in your truth, and teach me,
    for you are the God of my salvation,
    for you I wait all day long.
"Come," my heart says, "seek his face!"
    Your face, LORD, do I seek.
Give ear to my words, O LORD;
    give heed to my sighing
Listen to the sound of my cry,
    my King and my God,
    for to you I pray. Amen. (PSS 25:1, 4–5; 27:8; 5:1–2).

🖙 Allow some time for members to encourage one another to read the Devotional and Scripture Readings and do the exercise in the following chapter before the next meeting. Then invite the members to be silent for a few moments before leading them in reading the Closing Prayer aloud together.

🖙 At the end of the Closing Prayer, the leader asks for a volunteer to lead the next meeting.

## TAKING IT FURTHER

The next time you read a newspaper or watch the television news, try asking God some of the questions that come to your mind about the events and trends you see there.

ADDITIONAL EXERCISE

Donne, John. *Donne: Poems and Prose.* New York: Alfred A. Knopf, 1995.
Graham, Billy. *Just As I Am.* San Francisco: HarperSanFrancisco, 1997.

ADDITIONAL RESOURCES

Pinnock, Clark, and others. *The Openness of God: A Biblical Challenge to the Traditional Understanding of God.* Downers Grove, IL: InterVarsity, 1994.

Saint John of the Cross. *Dark Night of the Soul.* New York: Doubleday/ Image, 1959.

**ADDITIONAL REFLECTION QUESTIONS**

*What kind of attitude do you need to wrestle with God?*

*What distinction is there, if any, between wrestling with God and arguing with God?*

*How has God invited you to wrestle with him over situations in your life?*

# WALKING WITH GOD

## 12

**KEY SCRIPTURE: Genesis 6:9–22**

## DEVOTIONAL READING

GEORGE WHITEFIELD, "Walking with God," in *Whitefield's Sermons*

Genesis 5:24, "And Enoch walked with God: and he was not; for God took him."

First, Walking with God implies that the prevailing power of the enmity of a person's heart be taken away by the blessed Spirit of God. Perhaps it may seem a hard saying to some, but our own experience daily proves what the scriptures in many places assert, that the carnal mind, the mind of the unconverted natural man, nay, the mind of the regenerate, so far as any part of him remains unrenewed, is enmity, not only an enemy, but enmity itself, against God....

Secondly, Walking with God not only implies that the prevailing power of the enmity of a man's heart be taken away, but also that a person is actually reconciled to God the Father, in and through the all-sufficient righteousness and atonement of his dear Son....

Thirdly, Walking with God implies a settled abiding communion and fellowship with God, or what in scripture is called, 'The Holy Ghost dwelling in us.' This is what our Lord promised when he told his disciples that 'the Holy Spirit would be in and with them'; not to be like wayfaring man, to stay only for a night, but to reside and make his abode in their hearts....

Fourthly, Walking with God implies our making progress or advances in the divine life. Walking, in the very first idea of the word, seems to suppose a progressive motion. A person that walks, though he move slowly, yet he goes forward, and does not continue in one place. And so it is with those that walk with God....

How this is done, or, in other words, by what means believers keep up and maintain their walk with God, comes to be considered under our

> ✎ It is helpful for everyone to read the Devotional and Scripture Readings and do the My Life with God Exercise before the meeting. Begin the meeting with silent prayer, then move directly to Reflecting on My Life with God below.

*If you aren't moving up you are sliding down*

second general head. First, Believers keep up and maintain their walk with God by reading of his holy word.... Secondly, Believers keep up and maintain their walk with God by secret prayer.... Thirdly, Holy and frequent meditation is another blessed means of keeping up a believer's walk with God.... Fourthly, Believers keep up their walk with God, by watching and noting his providential dealings with them.... Fifthly, In order to walk closely with God, his children must not only watch the motions of God's providence without them, but the motions also of his blessed Spirit in their hearts.... Sixthly, They that would maintain a holy walk with God must walk with him in ordinances as well as providences.... Seventh and lastly, If you would walk with God, you will associate and keep company with those that do walk with him.[1]

## MY LIFE WITH GOD EXERCISE

Of course, as George Whitefield explains, walking with God is much more than the physical act of walking. But we can explore the idea of walking with God a little more closely by practicing "walking meditation." Set aside a period of time each day to walk prayerfully. If you can, choose a quiet place where you are not likely to run into neighbors or be bothered by a lot of traffic. (If the weather prevents you from walking outside, find a quiet place indoors to walk—perhaps in a public building or a covered walkway.) Walk slowly, even strolling. This is not an exercise walk. Think of the walk as an appointment you have each day to meet God. Start out by greeting God and thanking him for the blessings in your life, bringing to him any concerns you have—just as you do in your usual prayer time. But then move into thinking about the concept of walking with God. Ask God to help you to understand what it means to walk with him. Think about the forward motion of your walk. Look back over your life and consider those times when you felt as if you were moving forward with God and those times when you felt stalled or even that you were regressing. God may lead your thoughts down paths you don't expect. Allow for these "digressions," but if you find yourself becoming distracted by your to-do list or by the noises around you, repeat to yourself, "Lord, guide my steps" to focus your thoughts on God.

As the days wear on, start to pray about the progress you're making in your relationship with God. Ask God to help you reach the goals Whitefield described: to eradicate enmity from your heart, to totally reconcile yourself to him, and to fill you with the Holy Spirit. Read and reread the Devotional Reading before each walk. You might want to focus each time on one of Whitefield's aspects of walking with God, or just bring those things to God that stand out to you in the reading. For example: Are you surrounding yourself with those who keep company with God? Are you spending enough time studying his Word? Are you watching for him in the world around you?

*What did you learn about yourself and your relationship with the Lord during your conversational walks?*

**REFLECTING ON MY LIFE WITH GOD**
Allow each member a few moments to answer this question.

## ➤ SCRIPTURE READING: GENESIS 6:9–22

These are the descendants of Noah. Noah was a righteous man, blameless in his generation; Noah walked with God. And Noah had three sons, Shem, Ham, and Japheth.

    Now the earth was corrupt in God's sight, and the earth was filled with violence. And God saw that the earth was corrupt; for all flesh had corrupted its ways upon the earth. And God said to Noah, "I have determined to make an end of all flesh, for the earth is filled with violence because of them; now I am going to destroy them along with the earth. Make yourself an ark of cypress wood; make rooms in the ark, and cover it inside and out with pitch. This is how you are to make it: the length of the ark three hundred cubits, its width fifty cubits, and its height thirty cubits. Make a roof for the ark, and finish it to a cubit above; and put the door of the ark in its side; make it with lower, second, and third decks. For my part, I am going to bring a flood of waters on the earth, to destroy from under heaven all flesh in which is the breath of life; everything that is on the earth shall die. But I will establish my covenant with you; and you shall come into the ark, you, your sons, your wife, and your sons' wives with you. And of every living thing, of all flesh, you shall bring two of every kind into the ark, to keep them alive with you; they shall be male and female. Of the birds according to their kinds, and of the animals according to their kinds, of every creeping thing of the ground according to its kind, two of every kind shall come in to you, to keep them alive. Also take with you every kind of food that is eaten, and store it up; and it shall serve as food for you and for them." Noah did this; he did all that God commanded him.

✍ After everyone has had a chance to respond to the question, ask a member to read this passage from Scripture.

REFLECTION QUESTION
Allow each person a few
moments to respond to
this question.

*How does Noah walk with God?*

## ➤➤ GETTING THE PICTURE

After a brief discus-
sion, choose one person
to read this section.

*[handwritten note: Ark is archetype of Christ —]*

In the short term, the story of Noah is fairly simple: he builds a boat large enough to hold himself and his family, along with seven pairs of every clean animal and bird, and one pair of every unclean animal that lives on the dry land of the earth. After the boat is done, the people and creatures go inside and God shuts the door. "The fountains of the great deep burst forth, and the windows of the heavens were opened" for forty days and nights (Gen 7:11b–12). The waters rise, and the ark floats on their surface. "At the end of one hundred fifty days the waters had abated" (8:3b). Approximately three months later, Noah sends out birds to find out if there is any dry land—first a raven, then a dove. On the day that the dove doesn't return, he knows that "the waters were dried up from the earth." Two months later, it is totally dry (v 14). "So Noah went out with his sons and his wife and his sons' wives. And every animal, every creeping thing, and every bird, everything that moves on the earth, went out of the ark by families" (vv 18–19).

In the long term, however, the story is much more complex. The account in Scripture describes Noah's world as a place where "the wickedness of humankind was great ... and that every inclination of the thoughts of their hearts was only evil continually" (6:5). It doesn't take much imagination to create a picture of that continual and unrestrained evil—covetousness, malice, envy, murder, strife, deceit, craftiness, gossip, slander, idol worship, insolence, pride, rebellion, and so on—all and probably more than the apostle Paul lists in Romans 1:29–31. In the middle of this culture is Noah, a "preacher of righteousness" (2 Pet 2:5, NASB). Those of us who have been around people who choose not to acknowledge God and be answerable to God for their actions know that they carry their antipathy over to God's representatives. Their reactions to preachers are predictable: they demean them, call them hypocrites, portray them as fools. We can imagine that Noah's neighbors had the same reaction toward him when he called on them to repent and follow God.

And then God commands Noah to build an ark. Not only does he ask Noah to build a ship in the middle of a desert, but God asks for much more than a simple rowboat. Depending on the length of a cubit, the ark is to be as long as a medium-sized cruise ship or military destroyer (450 to 600 feet), twice as wide (75 to 100 feet), and taller than a four-story building (45 to 60 feet). Each of the three decks is to be at least one and one-half times the length of an American football field minus the end zones and approximately half as wide. In addition, Noah's family and the creatures need enormous amounts of food to sustain them for the months they were to be cooped up inside the ark. To secure the wood and pitch to make the ark and procure and store food for themselves and the creatures would have been a huge task that their neighbors would have watched and, doubtless, ridiculed.

### ▶▶▶ GOING DEEPER

Several traits in Noah help us understand why he is described in the Bible as having "walked with God." First and foremost, Noah had an unshakeable faith in God. Noah believed God. The author of Hebrews writes about him, "By faith Noah, warned by God about events as yet unseen, respected the warning and built an ark to save his household; by this he condemned the world and became an heir to the righteousness that is in accordance with faith" (11:7). He is listed in that "Faith Hall of Fame" as a person who had faith, "the assurance of things hoped for, the conviction of things not seen" (11:1). All of Noah's other traits follow from his strong faith.

*Have another member read this section.*

Second, he was obedient. Four times the word *commanded* is used when describing Noah: Genesis 6:22, "He did all that God commanded him"; 7:5, "Noah did all that the LORD had commanded him"; 7:9, ". . . as God had commanded Noah"; and 7:16, ". . . as God had commanded him." Noah was obedient to the call of God not only to be a herald of righteousness, but also when God asked him to do something that would make him look like a fool to the rest of the world.

Third, Noah was steadfast and patient. Building the ark was no small task. With hundreds of people working on it, the construction of a steel ship the size of the ark takes several years. The Bible suggests that it took Noah and his family twelve decades to build and stock the wooden ark. That is the supreme example of steadfastness and patience.

Fourth, to do what he did, Noah had to be completely reliant on and secure in God. There could be no wavering, no faltering from doing the task at hand. It makes us wonder if Noah knew before he started building how big the project was that he had been commanded to undertake!

Many of us have worked on one small part of a big project but would be totally overwhelmed if we were responsible for doing the whole thing. We aren't secure in our own knowledge or abilities because we rely on ourselves. Noah didn't have to rely on himself because he knew that God was in control and would help him. For Noah, walking with God meant relying on God, trusting God, and most of all, believing in God.

**REFLECTION QUESTION**
Allow each person a few moments to respond.

*How do you think you would react if God asked you to accomplish such a task?*

## ▶▶▶▶ POINTING TO GOD

🕊 Choose one member to read this section.

Like Noah, Christians throughout history who walked with God have had to remain out of step with society. One example is George Fox, the seventeenth-century founder of the Quakers. His Christian beliefs—that anyone, including women, could minister with the help of the Holy Spirit; that one was saved by belief alone and not by ritual; that church buildings were unnecessary, since God dwelled in the heart of his followers—were out of step even with the dissenters of his time. He and his followers, the Society of Friends, were persecuted and even imprisoned for their beliefs. But the more alone Fox felt and the more society rejected him, the closer he became to God, as this passage from his autobiography attests:

> But as I had forsaken the priests, so I left the separate preachers also, and those esteemed the most experienced people; for I saw there was none among them all that could speak to my condition. When all my hopes in them and in all men were gone, so that I had nothing outwardly to help me, nor could I tell what to do, then, oh, then, I heard a voice which said, 'There is one, even Christ Jesus, that can speak to thy condition'; and when I heard it, my heart did leap for joy.
>
> Then the Lord let me see why there was none upon the earth that could speak to my condition, namely, that I might give Him all the glory. For all are concluded under sin, and shut up in unbelief, as I had been; that Jesus Christ might have the pre-eminence who enlightens, and gives grace, and faith, and power. Thus when God doth work, who shall hinder it? and this I knew experimentally.
>
> My desire after the Lord grew stronger, and zeal in the pure knowledge of God, and of Christ alone, without the help of any

man, book, or writing. For though I read the Scriptures that spoke of Christ and of God, yet I knew Him not, but by revelation, as He who hath the key did open, and as the Father of Life drew me to His Son by His Spirit. Then the Lord gently led me along, and let me see His love, which was endless and eternal, surpassing all the knowledge that men have in the natural state, or can obtain from history or books; and that love let me see myself, as I was without Him.[2]

Like Noah before him, George Fox learned that walking with God often separates us from the world around us, but the rewards are much greater than those the world offers. This was also true for Jesus Christ, the only perfect example we have of walking with God.

## ▶▶▶▶▶ GOING FORWARD

Walking with God is the goal of all Christian life. It is the goal of all the ways we connect with God. In this book, we have looked at many different ways God communicates with us as we live with him. All of these means of communication, from praying to sensing God's presence to experiencing him in dreams and visions, are tools to help us better walk with God. Walking with God is spending time in his presence, moving forward with him in a spirit of companionship but also of apprenticeship, being willing to go where he leads. This ever-progressing relationship must always be the focus of our attempts to connect with and open ourselves to God.

Have another person read this section.

But walking with God is not easy; it takes time and experience to reach this intimacy with God as we journey through life. Some of us are beginners, others are further down the path. But all of us know where to look for instruction: Jesus was the only human who achieved perfect intimacy with God. Although the exact wording is never used in Scripture, no one could have been said to walk more closely with God than Jesus, God's son and a member of the Trinity.

All we need to learn about walking with God we can find in Jesus's life. He spent time with God in prayer, often going off alone to do so. His knowledge of the Scriptures was formidable, but he also knew that the letter of the law was not the most important thing, as exemplified by many stories about him, such as his healings on the Sabbath. He demonstrated a love for all people, including those thought untouchable and especially those who occupied the lowest rungs of society—orphans, widows, and the poor. In all things, he pointed to God the Father.

Truly, he exemplified Micah 6:8: "He has told you, O mortal, what is good; and what does the LORD require of you but to do justice, and to love kindness, and to walk humbly with your God?" Can we desire to do less?

*How else does Jesus's life demonstrate what it means to walk with God?*

**REFLECTION QUESTION**
Again, allow each member a few moments to answer this question.

After everyone has had a chance to respond, remind them that this is the last lesson in the book and ask the group if they would like to continue meeting. If everyone agrees to continue, this would be a good time to discuss when to meet and what material to use. When everyone has shared, the leader asks the members to be silent for a few moments before leading them in reading the Closing Prayer aloud together.

## CLOSING PRAYER

To you, O LORD, I lift up my soul.
Make me to know your ways, O LORD;
    teach me your paths.
Lead me in your truth, and teach me,
    for you are the God of my salvation,
    for you I wait all day long.
"Come," my heart says, "seek his face!"
    Your face, LORD, do I seek.
Give ear to my words, O LORD;
    give heed to my sighing.
Listen to the sound of my cry,
    my King and my God,
    for to you I pray. Amen. (PSS 25:1, 4–5; 27:8; 5:1–2)

## TAKING IT FURTHER

**ADDITIONAL EXERCISE**

Study this song by William Cowper. What does it teach you about walking with God?

### "Walking With God"—Genesis 5:24

Oh! for a closer walk with God,
A calm and heav'nly frame;
A light to shine upon the road
That leads me to the Lamb!

Where is the blessedness I knew
When first I saw the Lord?
Where is the soul-refreshing view
Of Jesus and his word?

What peaceful hours I once enjoy'd!
How sweet their memory still!
But they have left an aching void,
The world can never fill.

Return, O holy Dove, return!
Sweet messenger of rest!
I hate the sins that made thee mourn,
And drove thee from my breast.

The dearest idol I have known,
Whate'er that idol be,
Help me to tear it from thy throne,
And worship only thee.

So shall my walk be close with God,
Calm and serene my frame;
So purer light shall mark the road
That leads me to the Lamb.[3]

ADDITIONAL RESOURCES

Fox, George. *The Journal of George Fox*. Edited by Rufus M. Jones. Richmond, IN: Friends United Press, 1976.

Whitefield, George. *Whitefield's Sermons*. Grand Rapids, MI: Eerdmans, 1964.

ADDITIONAL REFLECTION QUESTIONS

*Francis of Assisi described himself as a fool for God, just as Noah's neighbors probably described Noah. How in your life have you been a fool for God? Or how have you been too embarrassed to be seen that way?*

Rm 1:16 fu I am
not ashamed of
the Gospel

*What qualities does Noah demonstrate among those described by Whitefield? What other characteristics do you think it takes to walk with God?*

Faithfulness, focus, listening to God, not deductive

*How have others in your life taught you what it means to walk with God?*

by Example, wibee w/ husbands, especially through hard times, deaths, etc.

# NOTES

## CHAPTER 1: LIVING WITH GOD

1. Frank C. Laubach, *Letters by a Modern Mystic* (Syracuse, NY: New Readers Press, 1979), 22–23.
2. Dallas Willard. *Hearing God: Developing a Conversational Relationship with God,* 3d ed. (Downers Grove, IL: InterVarsity, 1999), 18.
3. Frank C. Laubach, *Forty Years with the Silent Billion* (Old Tappan, NJ: Revell, 1970), 421.

## CHAPTER 2: TALKING WITH GOD

1. Jean-Nicholas Grou, *How to Pray* (Cambridge: James Clarke, 1955), 48–49.
2. Dallas Willard, *The Divine Conspiracy* (San Francisco: HarperSanFrancisco, 1988), 188.
3. George Müller, *Answers to Prayer* (Chicago: Moody Press, 1980), 17–18, 95–96.
4. Charles R. Parsons, *An Hour with George Mueller: The Man of Faith to Whom God Gave Millions,* 1897, available at http://www.charityministries.org/textonly/July2003-georgemueller.doc.
5. Eugene Peterson, *The Message // Remix* (Colorado Springs: NavPress, 1993), 1775.

## CHAPTER 3: MEETING GOD IN SCRIPTURE

1. Richard J. Foster and others, eds., *The Renovaré Spiritual Formation Bible* (San Francisco: HarperSanFrancisco, 2005), xxvii–xxviii.
2. Howard R. Macy, "Introduction to Psalms," *The Renovaré Spiritual Formation Bible* (San Francisco: HarperSanFrancisco, 2005), 776.
3. Augustine, *Confessions,* Bk. VIII, trans. and ed. Albert C. Outler (Philadelphia: Westminster Press, 1955), 213–14.
4. Willard, *Hearing God,* 107.

## CHAPTER 4: LISTENING TO GOD THROUGH THE CREATION

1. Francis of Assisi, *Francis and Clare: The Complete Writings,* trans. Regis J. Armstrong and Ignatius C. Brady (New York: Paulist, 1982), 38–39.
2. Brother Ugolino, *The Little Flowers of St. Francis of Assisi* (Grand Rapids, MI: Christian Classics Ethereal Library, 1997), 75–77.

## CHAPTER 5: HEARING GOD THROUGH OTHER PEOPLE

1. Willard, *Hearing God,* 95–96.
2. Sheldon Vanauken, *A Severe Mercy* (San Francisco: HarperSanFrancisco, 1977), 84–85.
3. Vanauken, *A Severe Mercy,* 85.
4. Vanauken, *A Severe Mercy,* 92–93.
5. Joyce Huggett, *The Joy of Listening to God* (Downers Grove, IL: InterVarsity, 1986), 141.

## CHAPTER 6: PERCEIVING GOD IN CIRCUMSTANCES

1. Philip Yancey, *Finding God in Unexpected Places*, rev. ed. (New York: Doubleday, 2005), xii–xiv.
2. Catherine Marshall, *Something More: In Search of a Deeper Faith* (New York: Avon, 1974), 10.
3. Marshall, *Something More*, 19.
4. "Reflections: Quotations to Contemplate," *Christianity Today*, Sept. 4, 2000.

## CHAPTER 7: SEEKING GOD IN SILENCE

1. Thomas à Kempis, *The Imitation of Christ*, trans. William C. Creasy (Notre Dame, IN: Ave Maria Press, 1989), 49–50.
2. Thomas Merton, *Dialogues with Silence: Prayers & Drawings*, ed. Jonathan Montaldo (San Francisco: HarperSanFrancisco, 2001), 57.
3. Merton, *Dialogues with Silence*, xiii.

## CHAPTER 8: SEEING GOD IN DREAMS AND VISIONS

1. Saint Teresa of Avila, *The Life of St. Teresa of Jesus, of the Order of Our Lady of Carmel*, trans. David Lewis (New York: Benziger Bros., 1904), 149, 155, 156, 158, available at http://www.ccel.org.
2. Brennan Manning, *A Glimpse of Jesus: The Stranger to Self-Hatred* (San Francisco: HarperSanFrancisco, 2003), 30–31.
3. Thomas Merton, *What Is Contemplation?* (Springfield, IL: Templegate, 1950), 12–13.

## CHAPTER 9: SENSING GOD'S PRESENCE

1. C. S. Lewis, *A Grief Observed* (San Francisco: HarperSanFrancisco, 1961), 3, 5–7.
2. Chad Walsh, "Afterword," in *A Grief Observed* (New York: Bantam, 1961), 149–50.
3. Anne Lamott, *Traveling Mercies: Some Thoughts on Faith* (New York: Pantheon, 1999), 49–50.
4. Lamott, *Traveling Mercies*, 50.
5. *A Grief Observed* (HarperSanFrancisco), 62–63.

## CHAPTER 10: ENCOUNTERING GOD'S MESSENGERS

1. Corrie ten Boom, *The Hiding Place* (Old Tappan, NJ: Revell, 1971), 166–67, 191–92; *Tramp for the Lord* (Old Tappan, NJ: Christian Literature Crusade & Revell, 1974), 17–18.
2. Billy Graham, *Angels: God's Secret Agents* (Nashville, TN: W Publishing Group, 1995), 3.

## CHAPTER 11: WRESTLING WITH GOD

1. Billy Graham, *Just As I Am* (San Francisco: HarperSanFrancisco, 1997), 48–53.
2. Richard E. Hughes, *The Progress of the Soul: The Interior Life of John Donne* (New York: William Morrow, 1968), 15–17.
3. Hughes, *The Progress of the Soul*, 59.
4. Hughes, *The Progress of the Soul*, 226.
5. John Donne and William Blake, *The Complete Poetry and Selected Prose of John Donne & The Complete Poetry of William Blake* (New York: Random House, 1941), 323.
6. John Donne, *Donne: Poems and Prose* (New York: Alfred A. Knopf, 1995), 227.

## CHAPTER 12: WALKING WITH GOD

1. George Whitefield. "Walking with God," in *Whitefield's Sermons* (Grand Rapids, MI: Eerdmans, 1964), 16–21, available at http://www.eternallifeministries.org.
2. George Fox, *George Fox: An Autobiography* (Philadelphia: Ferris & Leach, 1903), 29–30.
3. From *Olney Hymns*, 1779, William Cowper and John Newton, co-authors (public domain).

# ACKNOWLEDGMENTS

The seeds of this book lie in the rich material found in *The Renovaré Spiritual Formation Bible,* so first we must acknowledge and thank the other editors of that project—Richard J. Foster, Gayle Beebe, Thomas C. Oden, and Dallas Willard. Lyle SmithGraybeal has greatly enriched this guide with both his enthusiastic wellspring of ideas and his patient editing. At HarperSanFrancisco Cynthia DiTiberio has also done a wonderful job with the editing of the manuscript. Michael G. Maudlin of HarperSanFrancisco, Richard J. Foster and Lyle SmithGraybeal from RENOVARÉ, and Kathryn Helmers of Helmers Literary Services first envisioned this series of spiritual formation guides, so we thank them for their support and encouragement as well as for the faith they had in us. Finally, we are especially grateful to our families, particularly our spouses, Phil Graybeal and Ryan Waterman, for their support, inspiration, and love.

*Lynda L. Graybeal and Julia L. Roller*

*Grateful acknowledgment is made to the following for permission to reprint material copyrighted or controlled by them.*

The Scripture quotations contained herein are from the *New Revised Standard Version* Bible. Copyright © 1989, 1993, by the Division of Christian Education of the National Council of the Churches of Christ in the United States of America. Used by permission. All rights reserved.

Excerpts taken from *Finding God in Unexpected Places* (Revised and Updated) by Philip Yancey. Copyright © 2005 by S.C.C.T. Used with permission of Doubleday, a division of Random House, Inc., 1745 Broadway, New York, NY, www.randomhouse. com. Reproduced in the UK and Commonwealth by permission of Hodder and Stoughton, Limited, 338 Euston Road, London, England, www.hodderheadline. co.uk.

# WHAT IS RENOVARÉ?

RENOVARÉ (from the Latin meaning "to renew") is an infrachurch movement committed to the renewal of the Church of Jesus Christ in all its multifaceted expressions. Founded by best-selling author Richard J. Foster, RENOVARÉ is Christian in commitment, international in scope, and ecumenical in breadth.

In *The Renovaré Spiritual Formation Bible,* we observe how God spiritually formed his people through historical events and the practice of Spiritual Disciplines that is The With-God Life. RENOVARÉ continues this emphasis on spiritual formation by placing it within the context of the two-thousand-year history of the Church and six great Christian traditions we find in its life—Contemplative: The Prayer-Filled Life; Holiness: The Virtuous Life; Charismatic: The Spirit-Empowered Life; Social Justice: The Compassionate Life; Evangelical: The Word-Centered Life; and Incarnational: The Sacramental Life. This balanced vision of Christian faith and witness was modeled for us by Jesus Christ and was evident in the lives of countless saints: Antony, Francis of Assisi, Susanna Wesley, Phoebe Palmer, and others. The With-God Life of the People of God continues on today as Christians participate in the life and practices of local churches and look forward to spending eternity in that "all-inclusive community of loving persons with God himself at the very center of this community as its prime Sustainer and most glorious Inhabitant."

In addition to offering a balanced vision of the spiritual life, RENOVARÉ promotes a practical strategy for people seeking renewal by helping facilitate small spiritual formation groups; national, regional, and local conferences; one-day seminars; personal and group retreats; and readings from devotional classics that can sustain a long-term commitment to renewal. RENOVARÉ Resources for Spiritual Renewal, Spiritual Formation Guides, and *The Renovaré Spiritual Formation Bible*—books published by HarperSanFrancisco—seek to integrate historical, scholarly, and inspirational materials into practical, readable formats. These resources can be used in a variety of settings, including small groups, private and organizational retreats, individual devotions, and church school classes. Written and edited by people committed to the renewal of the Church, all of the materials present a balanced vision of Christian life and faith coupled with a practical strategy for spiritual growth and enrichment.

For more information about RENOVARÉ and its mission, please log on to its Web site (www.renovare.org) or write RENOVARÉ, 8 Inverness Drive East, Suite 102, Englewood, CO 80112-5624, USA.

## Introducing a Guide to Deepening Your Spirituality

*Combining the depth of a study Bible with the warmth of a devotional Bible, this revolutionary resource will make Scripture come alive in your daily life.*

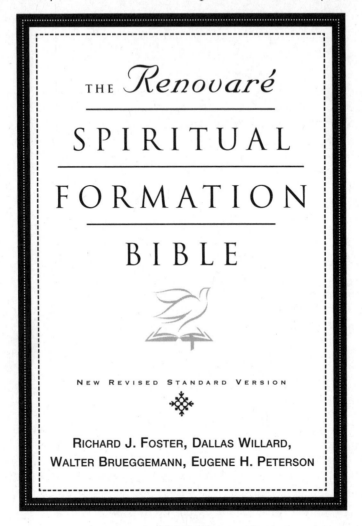

THE *Renovaré*

SPIRITUAL

FORMATION

BIBLE

NEW REVISED STANDARD VERSION

RICHARD J. FOSTER, DALLAS WILLARD,
WALTER BRUEGGEMANN, EUGENE H. PETERSON

Available Now

**THIS UNIQUE BIBLE FEATURES:**

The New Revised Standard Version • Fifteen progressive essays on living the "with-God life" • Introductions and notes for each book of the Bible, highlighting issues of spiritual formation and growth • Spiritual exercises • Profiles of key biblical characters • An Index that provides Bible references for each Spiritual Discipline • A Spiritual Formation Bibliography • Suggested Ways to Use This Bible for Spiritual Formation

0–06–067108–4 • $44.95/$59.50 (Can.)

**For more information on our books and authors visit www.authortracker.com.**